Site Carpentry and Joinery

Construction Competences for NVQ Level 2

LEEDS COLLEGE OF BUILDING LIBRARY
NORTH STREET
LEEDS LS2 7QT
Tel. (0113) 222 6097 and 6098

The NVQ Construction Series titles are:

A BUILDING CRAFT FOUNDATION by Peter Brett
(covers the five common core units)

SITE CARPENTRY AND JOINERY by Peter Brett
(covers the Site Carpentry units)

BRICKLAYING by W. G. Nash
(covers the Bricklaying units)

Site Carpentry and Joinery

CONSTRUCTION COMPETENCES
FOR NVQ: COMMON CORE

Peter Brett

BROOKLYN COLLEGE, BIRMINGHAM

Stanley Thornes (Publishers) Ltd

First published in 1993 by:
Stanley Thornes (Publishers) Ltd
Ellenborough House
Wellington Street
CHELTENHAM
Glos.
GL50 1YW
United Kingdom

99 00 01 / 10 9 8 7 6 5

A catalogue record for this book is available from the British Library

ISBN 0–7487–1298–4

Typeset by "Anneset", Weston-Super-Mare, Avon
Printed in Great Britain by Redwood Books, Trowbridge, Wiltshire

Contents

National vocational qualifications — NVQs

The work of a skilled person in the construction industry can be divided into various tasks, e.g. build a brick wall, paint a ceiling, hang a door, etc. These tasks along with many others are called **Units of Competence**. They can be considered as a 'Menu' for selection on a 'pick and mix' basis according to your requirements.

Traditional barriers to gaining a qualification such as age, length of training, mode of training, how and where skills are acquired, have been removed. You may train for NVQs in any order as, when and where you want.

Credits for Units of Competence which can be accumulated over any period of time, may be built into an NVQ award at three levels:

NVQ LEVEL 1   Competence in the performance of a varied range of work activities at a routine level. An introductory 'foundation' common core plus occupational-specific basic skills, e.g. wood, decorative or trowel occupations.

NVQ LEVEL 2   Competence in a significant range of varied work activities, some of which are complex or non-routine. A set of Units of Competence in a recognisable work role, e.g. bench joinery, carpentry and joinery (site practice), bricklaying, painting and decorating.

NVQ LEVEL 3   Competence in a broad range of varied work activities, most of which are complex or non-routine. An extension to the Level 2 Units of Competence to include additional skills, supervisory studies, quality control and assessment techniques.

NVQ qualifications in construction are jointly awarded by City and Guilds of London Institute (CGLI) and Construction Industry Training Board (CITB).

Prior achievement

It is not always necessary to undertake training for every Unit of Competence as colleges and other accredited centres will in future be able to undertake **Accreditation of Prior Learning/Achievement (APL/A)**. Through this process it is possible to gain credits for Units of Competence which have either formed part of another course you have studied, or are tasks you have previously carried out in industry.

You will need to produce evidence of the competence from past performance. This would then be taken into account when determining your training/accreditation programme and for the award of a qualification.

The advantages of this process are:
- increased motivation of trainees because there is no duplication of training previously carried out
- improved access to qualifications for experienced and mature trainees who have not had the opportunity to demonstrate their competences earlier.

A guide for lecturers, instructors and supervisors ('tutors')

An NVQ programme is unit-based. It needs to be flexible so that an employer or individual can specify a training and accreditation programme specifically to their requirements. Set length courses will become a thing of the past and a 'roll-on/roll-off' system of independent competency units, packaged according to employer or individual needs will come to the fore. Each unit is intended to be entirely free-standing with no prescribed order of attainment, time duration or start time. Therefore trainees with widely differing abilities and undertaking varying units, will have to be accommodated by the 'tutor'.

A trainee-centred learning approach using learning packages supported by tutor reinforcement and guidance is the ideal answer. It enables a flexible learning programme which caters for self selection, individual progression, mixed ability and 'roll-on/roll-off' programmes.

Using this method the trainees are made responsible for their own learning which is task orientated. The tutor's role changes to one of a facilitator, counsellor and assessor.

A Building Craft 'Foundation' and the follow-on *Construction Competences* series of craft/level specific packages provide a resource base for the implementation of NVQ Building Craft programmes within your training environment.

Introduction

The learning package you are about to start is one of the *Construction Competences* series. *NVQ Level 2 Site Carpentry and Joinery* is aimed at those working, intending to work or undergoing training as a carpenter and joiner. The workplace will be mainly on a building site and include new building work, maintenance, refurbishment and restoration. The successful completion of this package can be used as evidence of job knowledge achievement which, coupled with a demonstration of practical skills, can lead to the full NVQ Level 2 award.

The following eight units make up the NVQ Level 2 Carpentry and Joinery award:

Unit No. 58 Provide Surface Finishes (Internal and External Timber)

Unit No. 59 Install Finishing Components (Internal and External Timber)

Unit No. 60 Provide Dimensional Positioning for Setting Out Products (Basic Timber Components)

Unit No. 61 Assemble Components to Form Products (Basic Timber)

Unit No. 62 Install Structural Fabric Components (Vertical, Horizontal and Inclined Timber)

Unit No. 63 Produce Components from Procured Materials (Hand Fed Circular Rip Saw)

Unit No. 64 Install Structural Fabric Components (Roofs and Floors Timber)

Unit No. 65 Erect and Dismantle Access Platforms (Scaffolding)

The coverage of these Level 2 units in this learning pack has been arranged as far as possible using the accepted classification of a carpenter's and a joiner's work. To this end, some of the units have been grouped together. NVQ 2 unit numbers are indicated in brackets alongside the chapter title in the list below.

Unit 65 Erect and Dismantle Access Platforms (Scaffolding) does not appear in this learning pack. However, it is fully covered in *A Building Craft 'Foundation'* under 'Scaffolding', to which reference should be made.

Chapter 1 Basic Skills: A general study guide

Chapter 2 Joinery: Set out and assemble basic products (covers NVQ 2 Units Nos. 60 and 61)

Chapter 3 Woodworking Machining: Hand fed circular rip saw (covers NVQ 2 Unit No. 63)

Chapter 4 Carcassing: Install roofs and floors (covers NVQ 2 Unit No. 64)

Chapter 5 First Fixings: Studwork partitions, straight flight stairs, door linings and encasing services (covers NVQ 2 Unit No. 62)

Chapter 6 Second Fixings and Finishings: Install trim, doors, units, ironmongery, panelling and cladding (covers NVQ 2 Unit Nos. 58 and 59)

How to use this package

This is a self-study package designed to be supported by:
- tutor reinforcement and guidance
- group discussion
- films, slides and videos
- text books
- practical learning tasks.

You should read/work through each section of a chapter, one at a time as required. Discuss its content with your group, tutor, or friends wherever possible. Attempt to answer the *Questions for you* in that section. Progressively read through all the sections, discussing them and answering the questions and other learning tasks as you go. At the same time you should be either working on the matching practical learning task/assessment set by your college/training centre or, alternatively, be carrying out the practical competence and recording its successful completion in the workplace.

This process is intended to aid learning and enable you to evaluate your understanding of the particular section and to check your progress through the chapters and entire package. Where you are unable to answer a question, further reading and discussion of the section is required.

Throughout this learning package, 'Harry' the General Foreman will prompt you regarding important details.

The *Questions for you* in this package are either multiple choice or short answer.

Multiple-choice questions consist of a statement or question followed by four possible answers. Only **one** answer is correct, the others are distractors. Your response is recorded by filling in the line under the appropriate letter.

Example

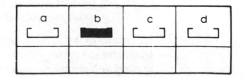

This indicates that you have selected (b) as the answer.

If after consideration you want to change your mind, fill in the box under your first answer and then fill in the line under the new letter.

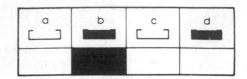

This changes the answer from (b) to (d).

Short-answer questions consist of a task to which a short written answer is required. The length will vary depending on the 'doing' word in the task, **Name** or **List** normally require one or two words for each item, **State**, **Define**, **Describe** or **Explain** will require a short sentence, **Draw** or **Sketch** will require an illustration. In addition sketches can be added to any written answer to aid clarification.

Example
Name the member used around frames to conceal the joint between wall and timber.

Typical answer: Architrave

Example
Define the term 'Herring-bone strutting'.

Typical answer: Diagonal cross-strutting fixed across joists at their mid-span to stiffen the joists and prevent lateral (sideways) movement.

Example
Produce a sketch to show the difference between herring-bone and solid strutting to floor joists.

Typical answer:

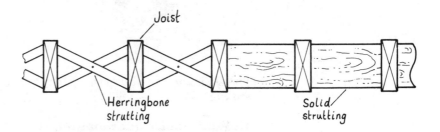

In addition this learning package also contains *Learning tasks*. Follow the instructions given with each exercise. They are intended to reinforce the work undertaken in this package. They give you the opportunity to use your newly acquired awareness and skills.

In common with NVQ knowledge and understanding assessments, the learning exercises in this package may also be attempted orally. You can simply tell someone your answer, point to a diagram, indicate a part in a learning pack or text book, or make sketches, etc.

1 Basic skills

READ THIS CHAPTER, WORKING THROUGH THE 'QUESTIONS FOR YOU'

In order to successfully complete the main practical activities in each Level 2 Unit of Competence, you will require an understanding of a range of enabling skills and supporting job knowledge, e.g. interpretation of drawings and oral/written instructions, adoption of safe working practices, loading and unloading materials, use of tools and general knowledge.

You may have already achieved some or all of these skills and knowledge either in industry or as a result of training at Level 1 or similar. Thus this basic skills chapter has been included in the form of typical questions for you to undertake. Questions are divided into topic areas. Where you cannot answer any particular question, further study should be undertaken using either the information source indicated, other appropriate text books, or talk it through with your tutor or a workmate.

This chapter should be studied on its own, or alongside other chapters according to your need.

Persons with prior achievement may wish to use these questions on basic skills as a refresher to support other chapters as required.

Interpreting instructions and Planning own work

These two topics are covered in *A Building Craft 'Foundation'* under 'Communications' and 'Materials'. These should be referred to if you have difficulty in answering the following questions.

Questions for you

1. State the reason why construction drawings are drawn to a scale and not full size.

_____

_____

2. Mark on the scale rule shown below 4.550 m to a scale of 1:50.

1:5 0	100mm	200	300	400	500	600	700mm
1:50	1m	2	3	4	5	6	7m

Metric   JAKAR   315 PL.   British Made

| 1:2500 | 20m | 40 | 60 | 80 | 100 | 120 | 140 | 160 | 180 | 200 | 220 | 240 | 260 | 280 | 300 | 320 | 340 | 360m |
| 1:1250 | 10m | 20 | 30 | 40 | 50 | 60 | 70 | 80 | 90 | 100 | 110 | 120 | 130 | 140 | 150 | 160 | 170 | 180m |

3. Produce sketches to show the standard symbols used to represent: brickwork, blockwork, concrete, sawn and planed timber.

THE TERMS 'UNWROT' AND 'WROT' ARE SOMETIMES USED INSTEAD OF SAWN AND PLANED TIMBER

4. State what is meant by orthographic projection.

_____

_____

5. Define the terms plan, elevation and section when applied to a drawing of an object.

_____

_____

_____

6. State the purpose of specifications and schedules.

_____

_____

7. State why messages must be relayed accurately.

_____

_____

8. State the meaning of the following standard abbreviations:

bwk _____   bldg _____

DPC _____   dwg _____

hwd _____   swd _____

9. State the action to be taken when damaged goods are received from a supplier.

_____

_____

10. State **ONE** reason why you as an employee should plan how to carry out work given to you.

_____

_____

11. Name the person you should contact in the event of a technical problem occurring at work.

_____

_____

12. State the reason why dust sheets should be used when working internally in occupied premises.

_____

_____

13. State why it is important to be polite with the customer.

_____

_____

REFER BACK TO THE INDICATED SOURCES IF YOU HAVE ANY PROBLEMS

14. State why it is important to be co-operative and helpful with work colleagues.

_____

_____

Adopting safe working practices

This topic is covered in *A Building Craft 'Foundation'* under 'Health and Safety' and 'Scaffolding'. These should be referred to if you have difficulty in answering the following questions.

Questions for you

15. State **TWO** duties expected of you as an employee under the Health and Safety at Work Act.

_____

_____

16. State **TWO** objectives of the Health and Safety at Work Act.

_____

_____

17. State **TWO** main powers of a Health and Safety Executive Inspector.

_____

_____

18. State **TWO** situations where protective equipment must be used. Name the item of equipment in **EACH** case.

_____

_____

19. State the reason for keeping work areas clear and tidy.

_____

_____

20. Name a suitable fire extinguisher for use on a flammable liquid or gas fire.

_____

21. Describe the correct body position for lifting a large box from ground level.

_____

_____

22. Name the type of safety sign that is contained in a yellow triangle with a black border.

_____

23. Describe the role of a site Safety Officer.

_____

_____

24. State the purpose of a toe board on a scaffold platform.

_____

_____

25. Name **TWO** parts of a ladder.

_____

26. List **THREE** checks that should be made before using a scaffold.

_____

_____

_____

27. State the correct working angle of a ladder.

_____

REFER BACK TO THE INDICATED SOURCES IF YOU HAVE ANY PROBLEMS

28. State the immediate action to be taken if a scaffold is found to be defective.

_____

_____

29. State where the flattened end of a putlog is inserted.

_____

Identifying, maintaining and using hand tools

This topic is covered in *Carpentry and Joinery for Building Craft Students*, Books 1 and 2. These should be referred to if you have difficulty in answering the following questions.

Questions for you

30. Produce a sketch to show the difference in cutting action between a rip and cross-cut saw.

31. Name the saw best used for cutting down the sides of tenons to a middle rail of a door.

_____

32. Define the difference between a warrington and claw hammer.

_____

_____

33. State an advantage of using a water level over using a spirit level.

_____

_____

34. State the procedure used for sharpening a plane iron.

_____

_____

35. When sharpening saws the following operations are carried out: setting, shaping, sharpening and topping. State the order in which these are carried out.

_____

_____

36. Explain the operations carried out when preparing a piece of sawn timber to PAR by hand.

_____

_____

37. State the purpose of using oil when sharpening plane and chisel blades.

_____

_____

38. Name the type of work for which a panel saw is most suitable.

_____

_____

39. Name the type of work for which a bullnose plane is most suitable.

_____

_____

40. Name **THREE** different types of chisel and state a use for **EACH**.

_____

_____

_____

41. State the purpose of a bradawl.

_____

42. Produce a sketch to show a mitre template and state a situation where it may be used.

_____

_____

43. Name a tool that can be used to draw large diameter curves.

_____

44. State the reason for taking off the corners of a smoothing plane iron after sharpening.

_____

_____

REFER BACK TO THE INDICATED SOURCES IF YOU HAVE ANY PROBLEMS

Setting up and using portable power tools

This topic is covered in *Carpentry and Joinery for Building Craft Students*, Books 1 and 2. These should be referred to if you have difficulty in answering the following questions.

_____ **Questions for you** _____

45. State **FOUR** basic safety rules that should be followed when using any powered tool.

_____

_____

_____

_____

46. When using a hand held electric circular saw state **THREE** operations that should be carried out before plugging the tool into the power supply.

_____

_____

_____

47. State the reason why power tools should never be carried, dragged or suspended by their cables.

_____

_____

48. Describe the procedure for plunge cutting with a jig saw.

_____

_____

49. State the reason why the cutters of a portable planer should be allowed to stop before putting the tool down.

_____

_____

50. State how cutters are held in a portable powered router.

_____

_____

51. Describe the **THREE** basic work stages when using a plunging portable powered router.

_____

_____

_____

52. Produce a sketch to show the correct direction of feed for a router in relation to the rotation of the cutter.

53. State the purpose of using 110 volt power tools.

_____

_____

54. What type of power tools do not require an earth wire?

_____

_____

55. State the correct location of an extension cable used in conjunction with a transformer that steps 240 volts mains supply down to 110 volts.

_____

_____

56. Which of the following sanders is best used for fine finishing work: circular, orbital, belt?

_____

57. A cartridge-operated fixing tool is to be used for fixing timber grounds to a concrete ceiling. List **THREE** items of equipment that are recommended for the operator to wear.

_____

_____

_____

58. The cartridge-operated fixing tool you are using on site has been supplied with **THREE** colours of cartridge: red, black and yellow. List them in order of decreasing strength.

_____

_____

_____

59. State the action that the operator should take if a power tool is not working correctly or its safety is suspect.

_____

_____

REFER BACK TO THE INDICATED SOURCES IF YOU HAVE ANY PROBLEMS

Handling timber-based materials and components

This topic is covered in *A Building Craft 'Foundation'* under 'Materials'. This should be referred to if you have difficulty in answering the following questions.

—————— Questions for you ——————

60. State the reason for stacking timber off the ground.

_____

_____

61. State **TWO** reasons why materials storage on site should be planned.

_____

_____

62. State **THREE** personal hygiene precautions which may be recommended by a manufacturer when handling materials.

_____

_____

_____

63. State the reason for using piling sticks or cross bearers when stacking carcassing timber.

_____

_____

64. Give the reason for stacking sheet materials flat and level.

_____

_____

65. Explain why joinery should be stored under cover after delivery.

_____

_____

66. State the reason why the leaning of items of joinery against walls is not to be recommended.

_____

_____

67. State the reason why new deliveries are put at the back of existing stock in the store.

_____

_____

68. Explain why liquids should not be kept in any container other than that supplied by the manufacturer.

_____

_____

69. Explain why veneered sheets of plywood are stored good face to good face.

_____

_____

REFER BACK TO THE INDICATED SOURCES IF YOU HAVE ANY PROBLEMS

General knowledge

1) Timber and manufactured boards
2) Preservatives
3) Adhesives
4) Fixings
5) Calculations

All topics except (5) are covered in *Carpentry and Joinery for Building Craft Students*, Books 1 and 2. These should be referred to if you have difficulty in answering the following questions. Calculations are covered in *Carpentry and Joinery for Advanced Craft Students: Site Practice*.

_____ **Questions for you** _____

70. Describe **THREE** main differences between softwoods and hardwoods.

_____

_____

_____

71. List **FOUR** common sawn sizes for carcassing timber.

_____

_____

72. Softwood is available in stock lengths from 1.8 m. State the measurement that stock lengths increase by.

_____

73. Produce a sketch to distinguish between multi-ply, blockboard and laminboard.

74. Describe what is meant by stress-graded timber and name **TWO** grades.

_____

_____

75. Produce sketches to show the following mouldings: torus, ogee, bullnosed, ovolo, scotia.

76. List the **TWO** initial factors that must be present for an attack of dry rot in timber.

_____

_____

77. Describe the **THREE** stages of an attack of dry rot.

_____

_____

_____

78. State the purpose of using preservative-treated timber.

_____

_____

79. Name **TWO** types of timber preservative and state **TWO** methods of application.

_____

_____

80. Produce sketches to show the following timber defects: cup shake, knot, cupping, waney edge and sloping grain.

81. Name **TWO** common wood-boring insects and for **EACH** state the location and timber they will most likely attack.

_____

_____

82. Define what is meant by conversion of timber and produce sketches to show through-and-through and quarter sawn.

_____

_____

83. Define the term seasoning of timber.

_____

_____

84. State a suitable moisture content when installing carcassing timber and explain how a moisture meter measures this.

_____

_____

_____

85. State **TWO** advantages that sheet material have over the use of solid timber.

_____

_____

86. A sheet of plywood has been marked up WBP grade. Explain what this means.

_____

_____

87. Explain the reason why water is brushed into the mesh side of hardboard prior to its use.

_____

_____

88. Define the following terms when applied to adhesives: storage/shelf life, pot life.

_____

_____

89. Explain the essential safety precaution to be taken when using a contact adhesive.

_____

_____

90. Produce a sketch to show the difference between countersunk, round-head and raised-head screws.

91. Describe a situation where **EACH** of the following nails may be used: wire nail, oval nail, annular nail and masonry nail.

_____

_____

_____

_____

92. Define with the aid of sketches **EACH** of the following types of nailing: dovetail, skew, and secret.

93. Describe a situation where a non-ferrous metal plug would be specified for screwing into rather than a fibre or plastic one.

_____

_____

94. Add together the following dimensions 750 mm, 1.200 m, 705 mm, 4.645 mm.

95. 756 joinery components are produced by a manufacturer. 327 are to be preservative treated, the remainder require painting. State how many are to be painted.

96. Nine pieces of timber are required to make an item of joinery. How many pieces of timber are required to make 17 such items?

97. A rectangular room measures 4.8 m × 5.2 m. Calculate the floor area and the length of skirting required. Allow for **ONE** 900 mm wide door opening.

98. Five semi-circular pieces of plywood are required. Calculate the cost of plywood at £4.55 per square metre if the radius of **EACH** semi-circular piece is 600 mm.

99. A 105 m run of carcassing timber is required for a project. You have been asked to allow an additional 15% for cutting and wastage. Determine the amount to be ordered.

100. A triangular piece of plywood has a base span of 1.4 m and a rise of 500 mm. Determine in metres square the area of five such pieces.

101. A semi-circular bay window has a diameter of 2.4 m. Determine the length of skirting required for this window.

102. A door 1980 mm in height is to have a handle fixed centrally. A security viewer is to be positioned 350 mm above this height. Determine the height of the viewer.

103. A carpenter earns £65.60 per day. The apprentice is paid 30% of this amount. Determine the wage bill for five days, for both people if the employer has to allow an additional 17.5% for on-costs.

104. Use a calculator or tables to solve the following:
(a) 457 divided by 239
(b) 6945 multiplied by 1350
(c) 336 raised to the third power
(d) The square root of 183.

WELL, HOW DID YOU DO?

REFER BACK TO THE INDICATED SOURCES IF YOU HAVE ANY PROBLEMS

2 Joinery

READ THIS CHAPTER, WORKING THROUGH THE QUESTIONS AND LEARNING TASKS

In undertaking this chapter you will be required to demonstrate your skill and knowledge of the following joinery processes:
- The setting out and assembly of basic joinery products.

You will be required practically to:
- Prepare setting out rods and cutting lists for a stormproof casement window and a framed, ledged and braced door.
- Mark out material for a stormproof casement window using pre-sectioned timber.
- Mark out material for a framed, ledged and braced door.
- Form joints, assemble and finish a casement window, including the hanging of sashes.

Production of joinery items

When making any item of joinery, various stages of work have to be carried out in order to complete the job. By adopting a methodical approach great savings can be achieved, both in time and prevention of costly mistakes.

The following workshop procedure checklist can be used to great advantage in both the hand and mechanised joiner's shop.

Workshop checklist

1) Prepare rod and cutting lists from scale drawing.
2) Select sawn timber from stock.
3) Plane timber on face sides.
4) Plane timber on face edges.
5) Plane timber to width.
6) Plane timber to thickness.
7) Mark out timber from rod.
8) Chop mortises.
9) Rip down the sides of the tenons.
10) Run square sections (rebates, plough grooves, etc.).
11) Run moulded sections.
12) Cut the shoulders of the tenons.
13) Fit the joints.
14) Assemble item dry. Check sizes, square and winding.
15) Clean up inside faces or edges of timber.
16) Glue up, re-check sizes, square and winding.
17) Clean up item.
18) Fit and hang any casements or cupboard doors.

Note: Stages 9 and 12 will, in mechanised shops, be carried out in one operation on a tenoning machine.

Workshop rods

Before making anything but the most simple one-off item of joinery, it is normal practice to set out a *workshop rod*. This is done by the 'setter-out' who translates the architect's scale details and specification into full-size vertical and horizontal sections of the item. In addition, particularly where shaped work is concerned, elevations may also be required. Rods are usually drawn on either thin board, thin plywood, white-painted hardboard or rolls of decorator's lining paper.

When the job with which they are concerned is complete and they are no longer required for reference, boards may be planed or sanded off and used again. Plywood and hardboard rods may be painted over with white emulsion. Although paper rods are often considered more convenient, because of their ease of handling and storage, they are less accurate in use. This is because paper is more susceptible to dimension changes as a result of humidity and also changes due to the inevitable creasing and folding of the paper. In order to avoid mistakes the critical dimensions shown in Figure 2.1 should be included where paper rods are used.

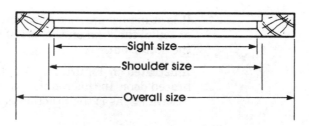

Figure 2.1 Critical dimensions

Sight size is the dimension between the innermost edges of the component, also known as daylight size as this is the height and width of a glazed opening which admits light.

Shoulder size is the length of the member (rail or muntin) between the shoulders.

Overall size (O/A) is the extreme length or width of an item.

Note: Where figured dimensions are different from the rod, always work to the stated size.

A typical rod for a casement window is shown in Figure 2.2. The drawings on the rod show the sections and positions of the various window components on a height and width rod. All of the component parts of the window can then be marked accurately from the rod. The rod should also contain the following information:
- Rod number
- Date drawn
- Contract number and location
- The scale drawing from which the rod was produced
- The number of jobs required

The drawing equipment the setter-out will use to produce the rod is also shown in Figure 2.2.
- A thumb rule for lines along the rod
- An adjustable bevel for splayed lines
- A try square for lines across the rod
- Dividers for spacing and curves

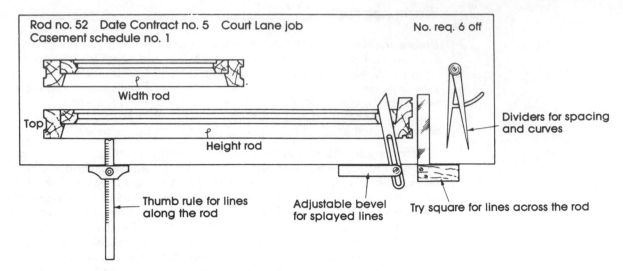

Figure 2.2 Rod for a casement window

It is standard practice to set out the height rod first, keeping the head, or top of the item on the left of the rod and the face of the item nearest the setter-out.

Illustrated in Figure 2.3 is a workshop rod for a framed, ledged and braced door. In this rod the position of the mortises have been indicated by crosses, as is the practice in many workshops.

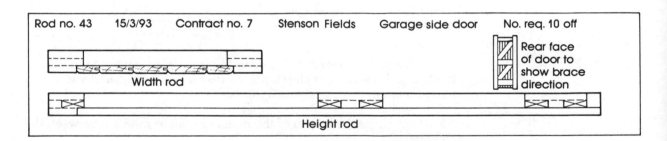

Figure 2.3 Rod for framed, ledged and braced door

Figure 2.4 shows the three easy stages which can be used to build up a detailed drawing. This method can be used when producing both workshop rods or scale drawings:
1) The components are drawn in their rectangular sections.
2) The square and moulded sections are added.
3) All other details are then added including hatching.

Note: The square and moulded sections should be the same depth. This eases the fitting of the joint as the shoulders of the tenon will be in the same position.

Sometimes it is not practical to set out the full height or width of very large items. In such cases the section may be reduced by broken lines and an add-on dimension inserted between them for use when marking out, as shown in Figure 2.5.

When determining details for doors and windows the setter-out must take into account their opening radius. A number of applicable door and window sections are illustrated in Figure 2.6.

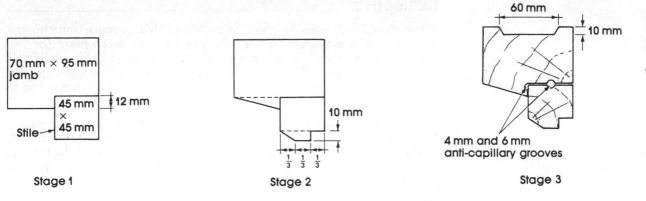

Stage 1 — 70 mm × 95 mm jamb; 45 mm × 45 mm Stile; 12 mm

Stage 2 — 10 mm; ⅓ ⅓ ⅓

Stage 3 — 60 mm; 10 mm; 4 mm and 6 mm anti-capillary grooves

Figure 2.4 Building up a drawing

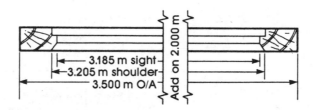

3.185 m sight
3.205 m shoulder
3.500 m O/A
Add on 2.000 m

Figure 2.5 Add-on dimensions

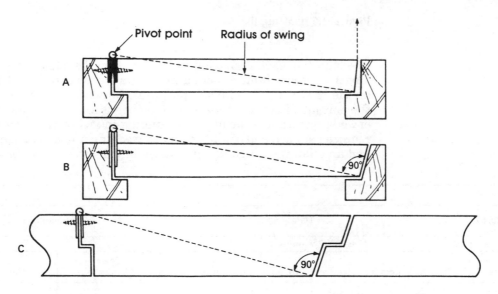

Pivot point   Radius of swing

A

B   90°

C   90°

Figure 2.6 Opening details (doors and windows)

Detail A shows that the closing edge must have a leading edge (bevelled off) to prevent it jamming on the frame when opened.

Detail B applies to the use of parliament and easy-clean hinges which both have extended pivot points. Here both the opening edge and frame jamb have been bevelled off at 90 degrees to a line drawn between the pivot point and the opposite inner closing edge.

Detail C shows how splayed rebates are determined for narrow double doors, bar doors and wicket gates, etc.

Cutting lists

When a rod has been completed the setter-out will prepare a cutting list of all material required for the job. The list will accompany the rod throughout the manufacturing operations. It is used by the machinists to select and prepare the required materials with the minimum amount of waste. The cutting list or a duplicate copy will finally be passed on to the office for job costing purposes.

There is no standard layout for cutting lists; their format varies widely between firms. However, it is important that the list contains details of the job, rod and contract in addition to a description of each item, the number required (No. off) and its finished size. Figure 2.7 shows a typical cutting list for six casement windows.

Cutting list		
Rod no. 52 Date		Contract no. 5
Job title Casement window		
Item	No. off	Finished size (mm)
Frame:		
jambs	12	70 × 95 × 1000
head	6	70 × 95 × 700
sill	6	70 × 120 × 700
Casement:		
stiles	12	45 × 45 × 900
top rail	6	45 × 45 × 500
bottom rail	6	45 × 70 × 500

Figure 2.7 Cutting list

The length of each item shown on the cutting list should be the precise length to be cut. It must include an allowance over the lengths indicated on the rod for manufacturing purposes. Between 50 mm and 75 mm is the normal allowance for each horn on heads and sills to take the thrust of wedging up and to facilitate its 'building-in'. A horn of at least 25 mm is required at each end of stiles for both wedging and protection purposes, and an allowance of 10 mm in length for rails that are to be wedged.

Cutting list					
Rod no. 52		Date		Contract no. 5	
Job title		Casement window			
Item no.	Item	No. off	Finished size	Sawn size	Material
	Frame:				
1	Jambs	12	70 × 95 × 1000	75 × 100 × 1000	Redwood
2	Head	6	70 × 95 × 700	75 × 100 × 700	Redwood
3	Sill	6	70 × 120 × 700	75 × 125 × 700	Oak
	Casement:				
4	Stiles	12	45 × 45 × 500	50 × 50 × 500	Redwood
5	Top rail	6	45 × 45 × 900	50 × 50 × 900	Redwood
6	Bottom rail	6	45 × 70 × 500	50 × 75 × 500	Redwood

Figure 2.8 Detailed cutting list

An alternative more detailed cutting list for the same six casement windows is shown in Figure 2.8. In addition to the previous one it contains the following information.

An *item number* that can be crayoned on each item to allow its easy identification during manufacture.

The *sawn sectional sizes* of the items to simplify the timber selection, sawing and final costing of the job.

The *type* of material to be used for each item e.g. softwood, hardwood or plywood, etc.

Marking out

After the timber has been prepared and faces marked, the actual marking out of the item can be done. This is the process of transferring the lengths, shoulder lines and mortises from the rod to the machined material.

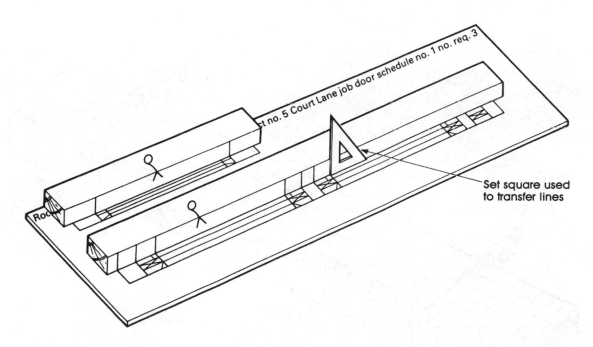

job door schedule no. 1 no. req. 3

...t no. 5 Court Lane

Set square used to transfer lines

Rod

Figure 2.9 Marking out from rod

A workshop rod for a glazed door is illustrated in Figure 2.9. It shows how a stile and rail are laid on the rod and the sight, shoulder and mortise position lines squared up with the aid of a set square. The mortises and rebates, etc. are set out as shown in the completed stile in Figure 2.10.

Stile rod 65

H M   M H M   Chamfer   M H M H

Rebate

Figure 2.10 Marked out stile

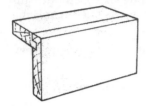

2 Joinery

Figure 2.11 Box square

In many joiners' shops it is standard practice to sketch the section on a member to enable all who handle it to instantly see how it should look when finished. Where a paired or handed member is required (stiles and jambs) the two pieces can be placed together on a bench with their face sides apart and the points squared over on to the second piece. Where pre-sectioned timber is to be marked out a box square, as shown in Figure 2.11, can be used to transfer the lines around the section.

Whenever more than one joinery item of a particular design is required, the first to be marked out becomes a pattern for the rest of the job. After checking the patterns against the rod for accuracy, they can be used to mark out all other pieces, and set up the machines. The positions of the mortises are normally marked out on all members, as it is not economical to spend time setting up chisel or chain mortising machines to work to stops, except where very long runs are concerned. Shoulder lines for tenons are only required on the pattern as tenoning machines are easily set up to stops enabling all similar members with tenons in a batch to be accurately machined to one setting. Figure 2.12 shows a pattern being used to mark out a batch of paired stiles. As any distortion of the timber could result in inaccuracies they must be firmly cramped together.

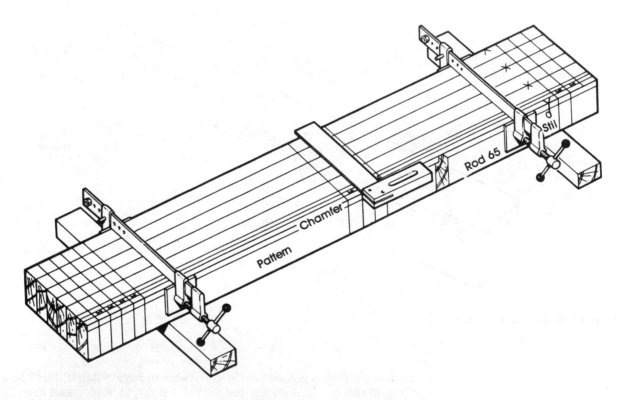

Figure 2.12 Marking out paired stiles from pattern

The use of this method ensures greater accuracy than if each piece were to be individually marked from the rod. Alternatively, a batch of stiles can be cramped between two patterns and the positions marked across with the aid of a short straight edge. At the end of a run the pattern can be machined, fitted and assembled to produce the final item.

Learning task

Draw to a scale of 1:2 the jamb of the door frame shown (draw the rectangular section first, then add the details).

Splay

9 mm dia anti—capillary groove

15 mm × 45 mm rebate

45 mm × 95 mm jamb

12 mm × 45 mm mortar key (central)

Casement windows

A **window** is a glazed opening in a wall used to admit daylight and air and also to give the building's occupants an outside view.

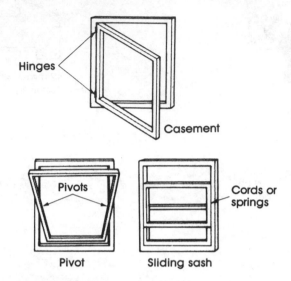

Figure 2.13 Types of window

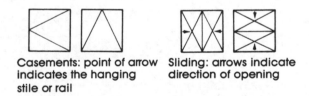

Figure 2.14 Direction of opening windows

A **casement window** is an opening window that is either top or side hung on hinges. It consists of two main parts: the frame and opening casement or casement sash.

The frame consists of head, sill and two jambs. Where the frame is subdivided, the intermediate vertical members are called mullions and the intermediate horizontal member is called a transom.

The opening casement consists of top rail, bottom rail and two stiles. Where the casement is subdivided, both the intermediate vertical and horizontal members are called glazing bars. Opening casements which are above the transom are known as fanlights. Fixed glazing is called a dead light and glazing at the bottom of a window, normally below a casement, is a sublight. Where glass is bedded in the main frame itself, it is called direct glazing.

The elevation of a four-light casement window is shown in Figure 2.15 with all the component parts named. The 'four' refers to the number of glazed openings or lights in the window.

Casement windows can further be divided into two types, traditional and stormproof depending on their method of construction.

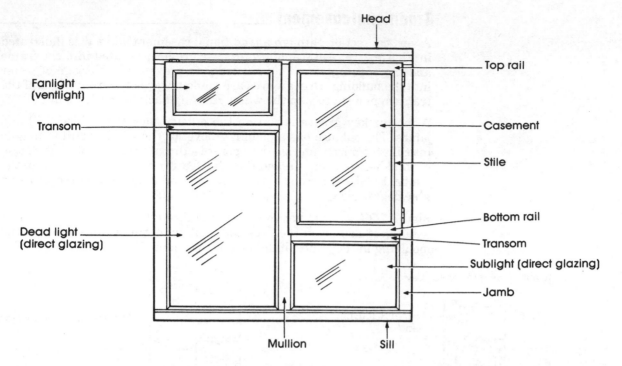

Figure 2.15 Four-light casement window

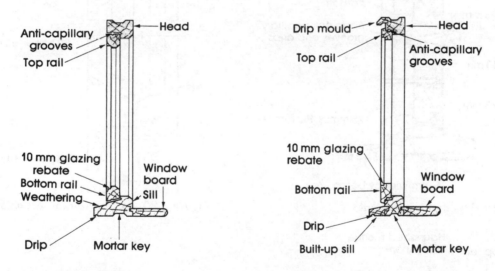

Figure 2.16 Traditional casement

Figure 2.17 Stormproof casement

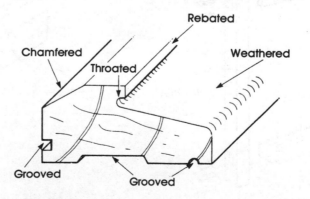

Figure 2.18 Application of standard profiles to a window section

Traditional casement

A vertical section through a traditional casement window is illustrated in Figure 2.19. Anti-capillary grooves are incorporated into the frame and the opening casements, in order to prevent the passage of water into the building. Drip grooves are made towards the front edges of the transom and sill to stop the water running back beneath them.

A mortar key groove is run on the outside face of the head, sill and jambs. The sill also has a plough groove for the window still to tongue into. Both transom and sill incorporate a throat to check the penetration of wind-assisted rain. In addition this feature may be continued up the jambs. Finally the front of the transom and sill is weathered: it has a nine degree slope for the rainwater to run off.

Figure 2.20 is a part horizontal section through a traditional casement window. It also shows the sizes and positions of the rebates, grooves and moulding in the jambs, mullion and casement stiles.

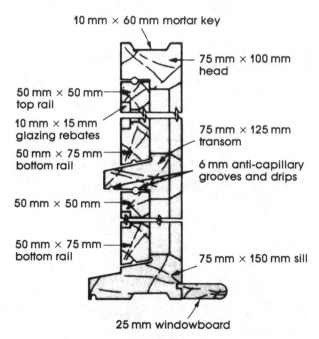

Figure 2.19 Traditional casement

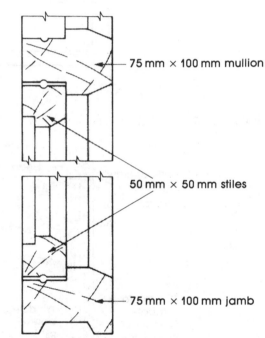

Figure 2.20 Part horizontal section of traditional casement

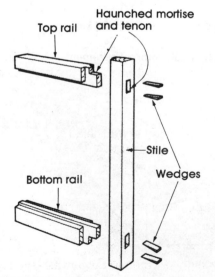

Figure 2.21 Haunched mortise and tenon joint, secured with wedges

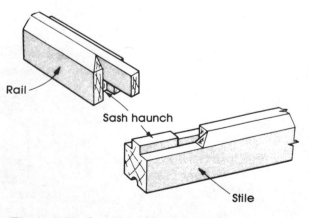

Figure 2.22 Joint detail (sash haunch)

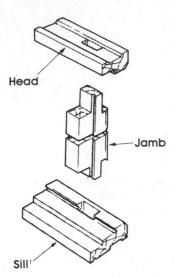

Head

Jamb

Sill

Figure 2.23 Jointing the frame

All joints used in traditional casement window construction are mortise and tenons. Standard haunched mortise and tenons (Figure 2.21) are generally used for the actual casements, although a sash haunch (Figure 2.22) is preferable where smaller sections are used. As a matter of good practice, the depth of the rebates should be kept the same as the depth of the mouldings. This simplifies the jointing as the shoulders of the tenons will be level.

The jointing of head, jamb and sill of the main frame are mortise and tenons (see Figure 2.23)). These joints are normally wedged, although the use of draw pins or star dowels is acceptable and even preferable where the horn is to be later cut off. In addition, by offsetting the hole in the tenon slightly towards the shoulder, the joint will be drawn up tight as the pin is driven in (see Figure 2.24).

In order to make a better weatherproof joint, the front edge of the transom is housed across the jamb (see Figure 2.25).

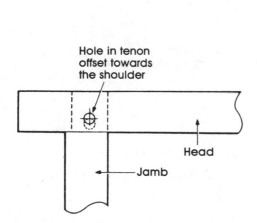

Hole in tenon
offset towards
the shoulder

Head

Jamb

Figure 2.24 Draw pinning

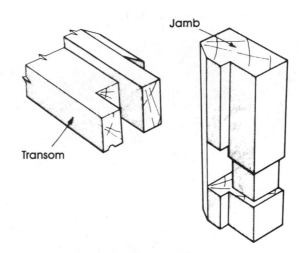

Jamb

Transom

Figure 2.25 Transom joint detail

Stormproof casement

Stormproof casement windows incorporate two rebates, one round the main frame, and the other round the casement. These rebates, in conjunction with the drip, anti-capillary grooves and throat make this type far more weatherproof than traditional casements (see Figure 2.26).

The jointing of the main frame of the stormproof casement window is often the same as that of the traditional casement, except for the transom which is not housed across the face of the jambs since it is usually of the same width. Comb joints can also be used, although they leave no horn for building in. Comb joints fixed with metal star dowels (see Figure 2.28) are normally used for jointing the actual casements, although mortise and tenon joints can be used.

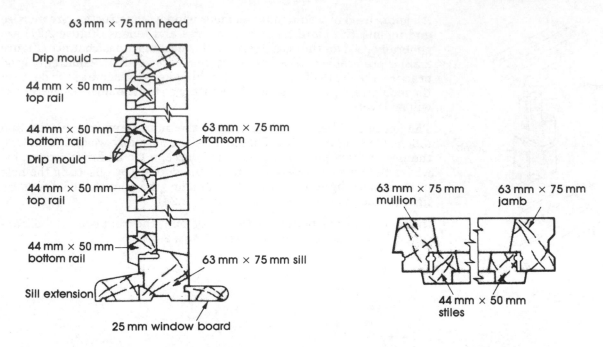

Figure 2.26 Stormproof casement

Figure 2.27 Part horizontal section of stormproof casement

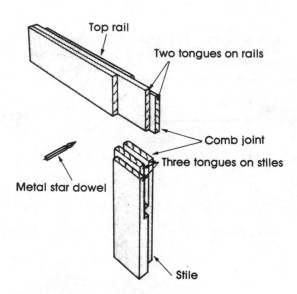

Figure 2.28 Comb joint secured with a metal star dowel

Assembly procedure

The main frame and casement should be assembled dry to check the fit of joints, sizes, square and winding.

Squaring up of a frame is checked with a squaring rod which consists of a length of rectangular section timber with a panel pin in its end as shown in Figure 2.29. The end with a panel pin is placed in one corner of the frame (see Figure 2.30). The length of the diagonal should then be marked in pencil on the rod. The other diagonal should then be checked. If the pencil marks occur in the same place, the frame must be square. If the frame is not square, then sash cramps should be angled to pull the frame into square as shown in Figure 2.31.

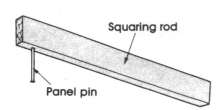

Squaring rod used to
check both diagonals

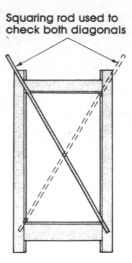

Figure 2.29 Squaring rod

Figure 2.30 Pulling the frame into square

ADJUSTMENT TO THE
JOINTS MAY BE
REQUIRED IF A
FRAME IS DISTORTED

Squaring rod used to
check both diagonals

Sash cramps
angled to pull
frame into square
if required

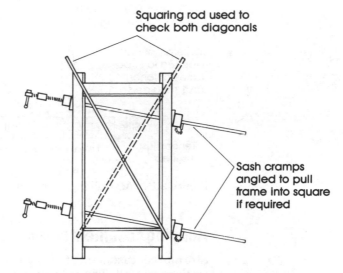

Figure 2.31 Pulling the frame into square using sash cramps

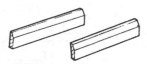

Figure 2.32 Winding strips

Winding of a frame is checked with winding strips (see Figure 2.32). These are two parallel pieces of timber. With the frame laying flat on a level bench, place a winding strip at either end of the job. Close one eye and sight the tops of the two strips as shown in Figure 2.33. If they appear parallel the frame is flat or out of wind. The frame is said to be winding, in wind or distorted if the two strips do not line up. Repositioning in the cramps or adjustment to the joints may be required.

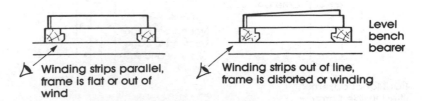

Winding strips parallel,
frame is flat or out of
wind

Level
bench
bearer

Winding strips out of line,
frame is distorted or winding

Figure 2.33 Check frame for winding

Glue up – assemble and lightly drive wedges. A waterproof adhesive should be used for external joinery or where it is likely to be used in a damp location. Ensure the overall sizes are within the stated tolerances. Re-check for square and wind. Assuming all is correct, finally drive wedges and insert star dowels as appropriate.

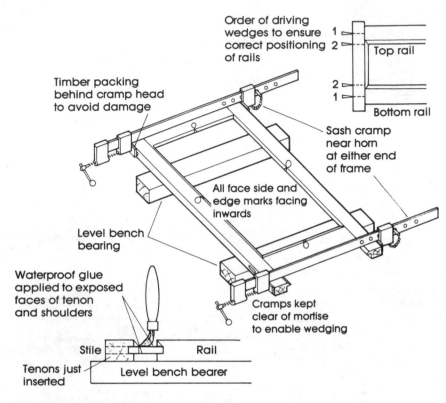

Figure 2.34 Assembling casement sash

Hanging casement sashes

Stormproof casements fit on the face of the frame and normally require no fitting at all. The only operation necessary to hang the casement is the screwing on of the hinges as shown in Figure 2.35.

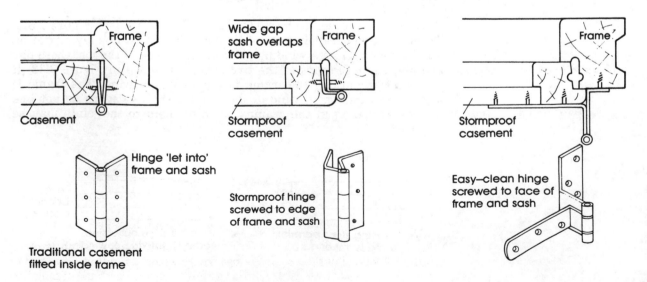

Figure 2.35 Hinging of casement sashes

However, traditional casements fit inside the frame and require both fitting and hanging. This is often thought of as a difficult task but by following the procedure given and illustrated in Figure 2.36, the task is greatly simplified.

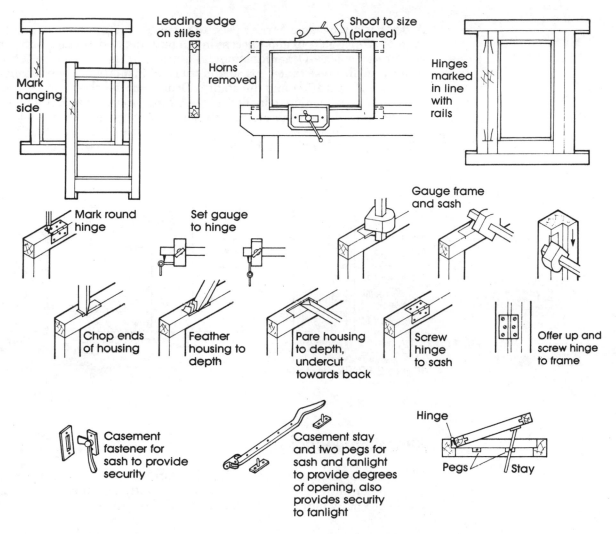

Figure 2.36 Fitting and hanging a casement sash

Fitting and hanging procedure

1) Mark the hanging side on both the sash and the frame.
2) Cut off the horns.
3) 'Shoot in' (plane to fit) the hanging stile.
4) Shoot the sash to width.
5) Shoot in the top and bottom of the sash.
6) Mark out and cut in the hinges.
7) Screw one leaf of the hinges to the sash.
8) Offer up the sash to the opening and screw the other leaf to the frame.
9) Adjust fit if required and fix any other ironmongery.

The two stiles when planed should have a 'leading edge' (slightly out of square). This allows the sash to close freely without binding. The joint on casements should be 2 mm. This is to allow a certain amount of moisture movement and not cause the casement to jamb in the frame.

Doors

A **door** is a moveable barrier used to cover an opening in a structure. Its main function is to allow access into a building and passage between the interior spaces. Other functional requirements may include weather protection, fire resistance, sound and thermal insulation, security, privacy, ease of operation and durability. Doors may be classified by their method of construction: panelled, glazed, flush, matchboard, fire resistant, etc., and also by their method of operation: swinging, sliding, folding or revolving. See *Carpentry and Joinery for Advanced Craft Students*: *Site Practice* for further information.

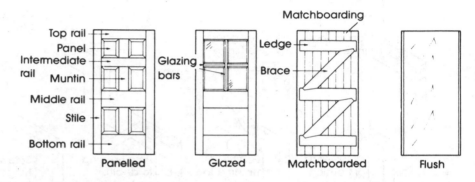

Figure 2.37 Types of door construction

Matchboarded doors

This group of doors involves the simplest form of construction. They are suitable for both internal and external use, although they are mainly used externally for gates, sheds and industrial buildings.

Ledged and braced door

The basic door shown in Figure 2.38 consists of matchboarding which is held together by ledges. This type is little used because it has a tendency to sag and distort on the side opposite the hinges. In order to overcome this braces are usually incorporated in the construction (see Figure 2.39). The use of braces greatly increases the rigidity of the door. The bottom ends of the braces should always point towards the hinged edge of the door in order to provide the required support. Where these doors are used externally, the top edge of the ledges should be weathered to stop the accumulation of rainwater and moisture (see Figure 2.40).

Three ledges are used to hold the matchboarding together. The outside pieces should be fixed with screws, while the remaining lengths of matchboarding are nailed to the ledges. Lost-head nails 6 mm longer than the thickness of the door are used for this purpose. The nails should be punched in and clenched over. Clenching over simply means bending the protruding part of the nails over and punching the ends below the surface as shown in Figure 2.41. The two braces, when used, are also fixed with lost-head nails which are clenched over. The joint detail between the ledges and braces is shown in Figure 2.42.

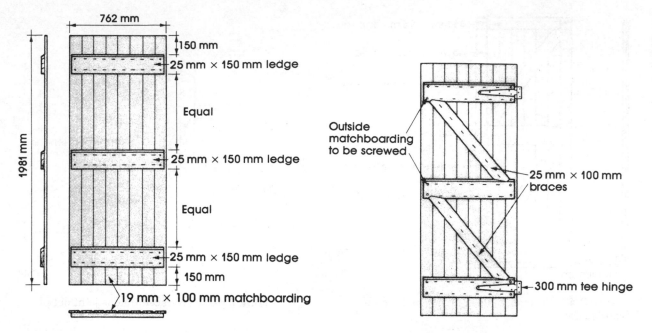

Figure 2.38 Ledged and matchboarded door

Figure 2.39 Ledged, braced and matchboarded door

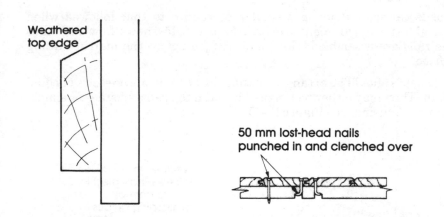

Figure 2.40 Weathering to top edge of ledges if door is for external use

Figure 2.41 Clenching over

Figure 2.42 Joint detail between ledges and braces

Framed, ledged, braced and matchboarded door

This type of door is an improvement on the ledged, braced and matchboarded door, as it includes stiles which are jointed to the top, bottom and middle rails with mortise and tenons.

The use of the framework increases the door's strength, and resists any tendency which the door might have to distort. Braces are optional when the door is framed, but their use further increases the door's strength.

Figure 2.43 shows that the stiles and top rail are the same thickness, while the middle and bottom rails are thinner. This is so that the matchboarding can be tongued into the top rail, over the face of the middle and bottom rails, and run to the bottom of the door. As the middle and bottom rails are thinner than the stiles, bare-faced tenons (tenons with only one shoulder) must be used (see Figure 2.44). These joints are normally wedged, although for extra strength draw pins can be used.

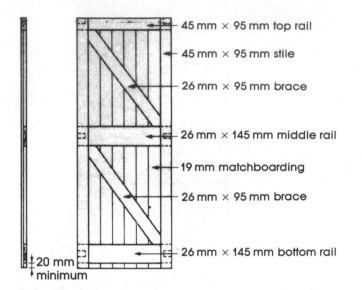

Figure 2.43 Framed, ledged, braced and match-boarded door

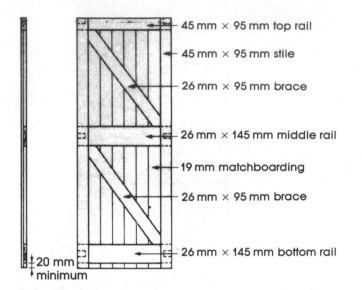

45 mm × 95 mm top rail

45 mm × 95 mm stile

26 mm × 95 mm brace

26 mm × 145 mm middle rail

19 mm matchboarding

26 mm × 95 mm brace

26 mm × 145 mm bottom rail

20 mm minimum

Figure 2.43 Framed, ledged, braced and match-boarded door

Bare-faced tenons

Draw pins

Figure 2.44 Bare-faced tenons joint detail

Assembly procedure for framed matchboarded doors

This is carried out using a similar procedure to that followed when assembling the casement window. Figure 2.45 shows how the stiles and rails are assembled, glued and wedged before the matchboarding is fixed.

The boards should be arranged so that the two outside ones are of equal width. They may either be tongued into the top rail and stiles or simply fit into a housing (see Figure 2.46).

DRIVE WEDGES IN THE ORDER SHOWN FOR CORRECT RAIL POSITIONING

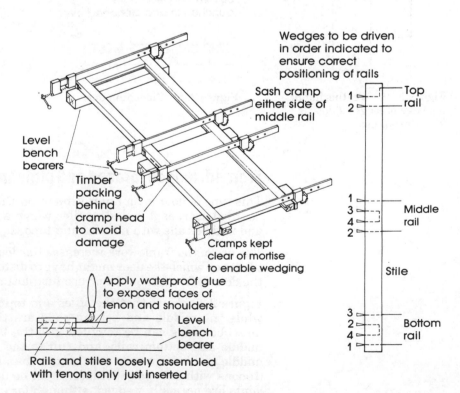

Wedges to be driven in order indicated to ensure correct positioning of rails

Sash cramp either side of middle rail

Level bench bearers

Timber packing behind cramp head to avoid damage

Cramps kept clear of mortise to enable wedging

Apply waterproof glue to exposed faces of tenon and shoulders

Level bench bearer

Rails and stiles loosely assembled with tenons only just inserted

Top rail

Middle rail

Stile

Bottom rail

Figure 2.45 Assembling framed matchboarded door

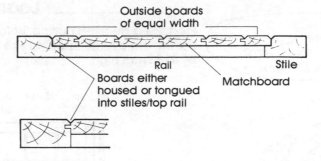

Figure 2.46 Matchboarding details

Before assembly the tongues and grooves, the backs of rails and braces and all other concealed surfaces must be treated with a suitable priming paint or preservative.

Arrange the boards on the assembled frame. Locate tongues and grooves so that the boards form an arc between the jambs. Place a short piece of timber across the door at either end. With assistance apply pressure at both ends of the door to fold the boards flat (see Figure 2.47).

Tap up the boards from the bottom to locate them correctly into the top rail and then clench nail or staple them (using a pneumatic nail gun) to all framing members.

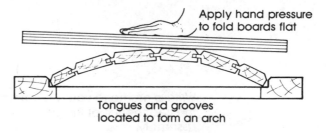

Figure 2.47 Folding matchboards

Mark, cut and fix the braces. These may be either cut into the corners of the framework, or let into the rails. The cut in the corner method is simpler, however, it has a tendency to push open the joints between the stiles and the rails.

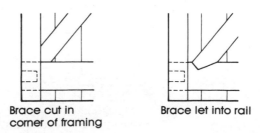

Figure 2.48 Fitting braces

READ THE INSTRUCTIONS AND COMPLETE THE TASK

Learning task

Produce a detailed cutting list for the pair of softwood garage doors shown. The overall opening size of the door frame is 2440 mm wide by 2135 mm high.

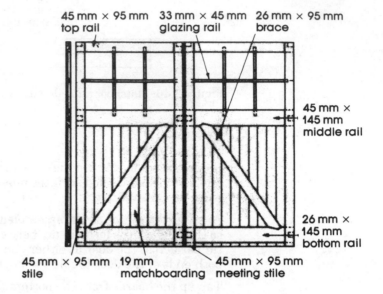

45 mm × 95 mm top rail

33 mm × 45 mm glazing rail

26 mm × 95 mm brace

45 mm × 145 mm middle rail

26 mm × 145 mm bottom rail

45 mm × 95 mm stile

19 mm matchboarding

45 mm × 95 mm meeting stile

Write a memo to your workmate, who is a new trainee, concerning the treatment that the prepared components require before assembly.

BBS CONSTRUCTION	**MEMO**
From _____	To _____
Subject _____	Date _____
Message	

TRY TO ANSWER THESE

Questions for you

1. Name the joint that is used between the stile and the middle/bottom rails of a framed, ledged and braced door.

_____

2. List **FIVE** items of information that can be obtained from a setting out rod.

_____

_____

_____

_____

_____

3. Name the type of tenon shown.

_____

4. Braces are incorporated into matchboarded doors in order to:
(a) provide a fixing for the hinges
(b) prevent the door from sagging
(c) joint matchboarding together
(d) protect the door from weather

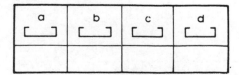

a	b	c	d
[ ]	[ ]	[ ]	[ ]

5. When making a window frame, the operation to be carried out directly after planing should be
(a) mark out timber
(b) chop mortises
(c) rip sides of tenons
(d) prepare rod

a	b	c	d
[ ]	[ ]	[ ]	[ ]

6. Explain why a workshop rod is drawn full size and not to scale.

_____

_____

7. Name a suitable piece of ironmongery for the fastening of
(a) a top-hung casement
(b) a side-hung casement sash

_____

_____

8. Name the intermediate vertical member used to divide a casement window frame.

_____

9. State the reason for draw-pinning mortise and tenon joints.

_____

_____

10. Produce a sketch to show the jointing arrangement between the brace and ledge of a matchboarded door.

11. Produce a sketch to show the difference between the sight size, shoulder size and overall size of a joinery component.

12. The marking-out tool used for squaring shoulders around pre-sectioned timber is:
(a) mitre square
(b) try square
(c) combination square
(d) box square

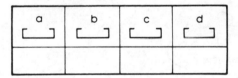

13. Produce a sketch to show the horn of the head of a casement window frame prepared ready for building in.

14. State the reason why the stiles of a traditional casement window sash are planed with a 'leading edge'.

_____

_____

15. The following operations are undertaken in the production of an item of joinery. Re-write the list in the order that they should be carried out:

1) chop mortises
2) fit joints
3) cut tenon shoulders
4) glue and assemble
5) mark out from rod
6) rip tenons
7) prepare rod
8) select timber
9) plane timber
10) run sections

Doors

WORD-SQUARE SEARCH

Hidden in the word-square are the following 20 words associated with '*Joinery*'. You may find the words written forwards, backwards, up, down or diagonally.

Joinery	Light
Casement	Barefaced
Sash	Rod
Traditional	Workshop
Matchboard	Cutting list
Stormproof	Window
Stile	Door
Rail	Squaring
Mullion	Winding
Jamb	Allowance

Draw a ring around the words, or line in using a highlight pen thus:

EXAMPLE

EXAMPLE

```
L A N O I T I D A R T K B G E W C M
R C K B C D R H L C D E F N G O X A
C D P E C C E A L I A R D I Y D Z T
U X O A A B L K O D E H A R K N W C
T A H C S E I B W O Q B O A A I B H
T R S B E K T C A E H D A U E W O B
I C K D M E S F N G I J L Q K M L O
N B R O E M C U C D P V S S X J P A
G D O K N T E E F W K C E O F P R
L E W M T B V C G I G X Z I F E Y D
I F I L S C A Z N P A C N B J F J K
S G J N S F O D K Q C E R B N A M L
T H H P E A I P O O R S T E F G M C
B C S R T N P D L Y D H I L K N B B
A D A O G E W E I E F B B C L R A C
E B S R H G Y F G F M U L L I O N B
G F H Q A F X J H C E M W A T O F E
F O O R P M R O T S G B J I V D H G
```

3 Woodworking machining

Read this chapter, working through the questions and learning tasks

In undertaking this chapter you will be required to demonstrate your skill and knowledge of:
- Using and maintaining a hand fed circular rip saw.

You will be required practically to:
- Use a hand fed circular rip saw complying with current regulations to produce sawn components: square, rectangular, bevelled, angled, wedged and tapered.

Hand fed circular rip saw

Figure 3.1 Rip saw

The main purpose of a rip saw is to resaw timber from its marketable sectional size into the required section.

This may involve:
- cutting the timber to the required width, known as *flatting*.
- cutting the timber to the required thickness, known as *deeping*.
- cutting the timber to the appropriate angle or bevel. Machine operators will make their own bed pieces and saddles which enable them safely to carry out angle and bevel ripping.
- cutting the timber to the appropriate taper or wedge shape. Machine operators will make their own push blocks having the required taper or wedge shape on their edge which enable them safely to carry out tapered ripping or wedge cutting.

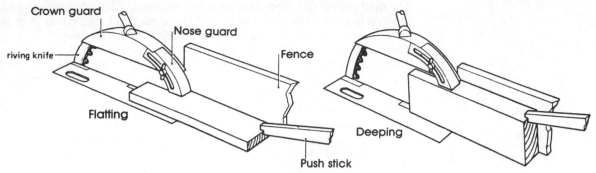

Figure 3.2 Flatting and deeping

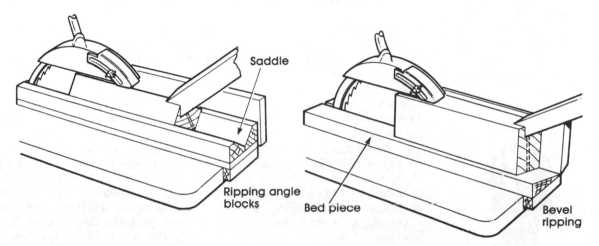

Figure 3.3 Bed pieces and saddles

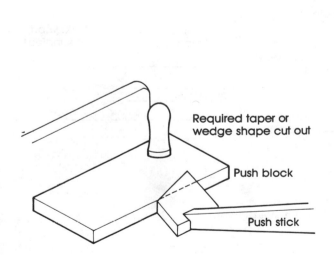

Figure 3.4 Use of push block to cut wedges

Figure 3.5 Parts of the rip saw

Figure 3.5 shows the following parts of the rip saw:

The *crown guard* (A) is vertically adjustable and when set up for sawing, it must completely cover the gullets of the top teeth.

49

The *nose guard* (B) should be adjusted for each cutting operation so that the gap between the nose guard and the material being cut is as close as practicably possible. A maximum of 12 mm is permissible.

The *pillar* (C) and adjusting handle for the crown guard.

The *riving knife* (D) rises and falls along with the saw when the depth of cut is altered. Whenever a saw blade is changed, the riving knife must be adjusted so that it is as close as practicably possible to the saw blade and, in any case, the distance between the riving knife and the teeth of the saw blade should not exceed 12 mm. It should be thicker than the saw blade as its purpose is to stop the material binding on the saw blade while being cut and also to guard the back edge of the saw blade.

The *fence* (E) is adjusted by slackening the hand lever and moving the fence on its slide to give the required width of cut. The fence should be set so that the arc at the end of the fence is in line with the gullets of the saw teeth at table level. This helps to prevent the timber binding on the saw blade.

The *knulled adjusting knob* (F), by rotation, gives a fine adjustment of the fence. The measurement between the saw blade and fence is indicated on the graduated scale above the slide.

The *rise and fall handle* (G) raises or lowers the blade.

Start and *stop* controls (H).

The *table groove* (I) enables a cross-cut guide or mitre fence to be used.

The *access cover* (J) is removed to give access to the spindle when changing saw blades.

The *finger plate* (K) is removed to give access to the spindle when changing saw blades. Some saws have a recess on each side of the blade where it enters the table. These recesses are to receive felt packings, a hardwood mouthpiece and a hardwood backfilling. The packings and backfillings prevent the saw being deflected and keep it cutting in a true line. The mouthpiece protects the packing from damage by the saw teeth and prevents the underside of the timber breaking out or 'spelching'. The backfilling also prevents damage to the saw teeth should it run out of true.

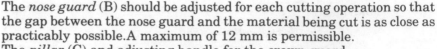

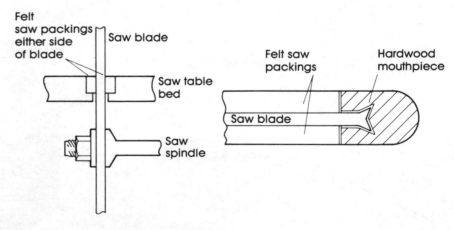

Figure 3.6 Saw packings and mouthpiece

Safety in operation

The safety requirements of the Woodworking Machine Regulations 1974 which are imposed wherever woodworking machines are in use may be summarised as follows:
1) The cutters of every machine must be enclosed by a substantial guard to the maximum possible extent.
2) In general no adjustment should be made to the guards or any other part of the machine while the cutters are in motion.
3) Every machine must have an effective starting and stopping device. This should be located so that it is easily used by the operator especially in the case of an emergency.
4) The working area around a machine must be kept free from obstruction, offcuts, shavings, etc.
5) The floor surface of the work area must be level, non-slip and maintained in good condition.
6) A reasonable temperature must be maintained in the workplace and in any case must not fall below 13°C or 10°C in a saw mill. Where this is not possible because the machine is situated in the open air, radiant heaters must be provided near or adjacent to the work area, to enable operators to warm themselves periodically.
7) No person must use any woodworking machine unless he/she has been properly trained for the work being carried out or he/she is under close supervision as part of the training.
8) Machine operators must:
   (a) Use correctly all guards and safety devices required by the regulations.
   (b) Report to the supervisor or employer any faults or contraventions of the regulations.
9) Any person who sells or hires a woodworking machine must ensure it complies with the regulations.

REFER TO THESE REGULATIONS

The safety requirements of the Woodworking Machine Regulations 1974 which are applicable to circular saws are:
1) The part of the saw blade which is below the saw table must be enclosed to the maximum possible extent.
2) A strong, adjustable riving knife must be fitted directly behind the saw blade. Its purpose is to part the timber as it proceeds through the saw and thus prevents it jamming on the blade and being thrown back towards the operator.
3) The upper part of the saw blade must be fitted with a strong adjustable crown guard which has flanges that cover the full depth of the saw teeth. The adjustable extension piece should be positioned to within 12 mm of the surface of the material being cut.
4) The diameter of the saw blade must never be less than $\frac{6}{10}$ (60 per cent) of the largest saw blade for which the machine is designed. In the case of a multi-speed machine the diameter of the saw blade must never be less than 60 per cent of the largest saw blade which can be properly used at the highest speed. A notice must always be fixed to each machine clearly stating the minimum diameter of the saw blade that may be used.
5) Circular saws must not:
   (a) Be used for cutting tenons, grooves, rebates or moulding unless effectively guarded. These normally take the form of shaw 'tunnel type' guards which, in addition to enclosing the blade, apply pressure to the work piece, keeping it in place.

(b) Be used for ripping unless the saw teeth project above the timber, i.e. deeping large sectioned material in two cuts is not permissible.

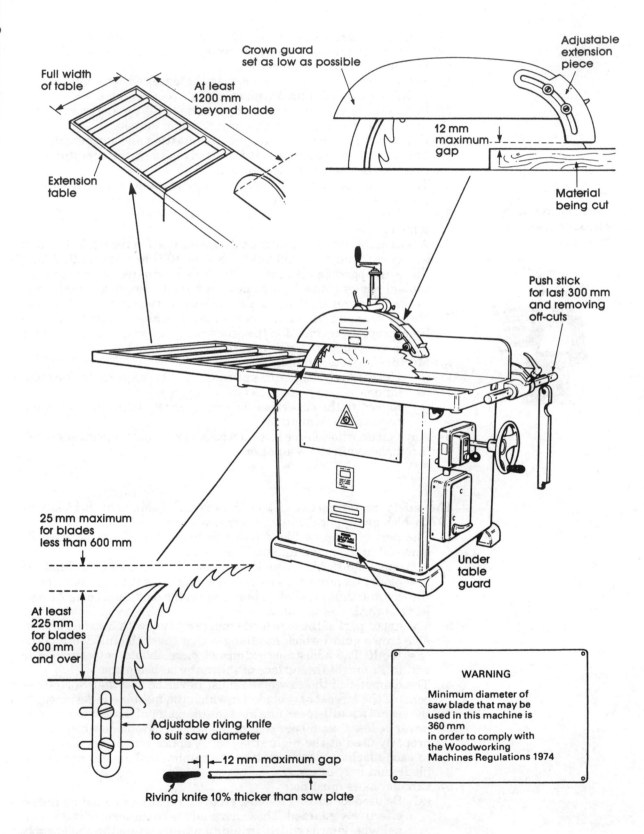

Full width of table

At least 1200 mm beyond blade

Extension table

Crown guard set as low as possible

Adjustable extension piece

12 mm maximum gap

Material being cut

Push stick for last 300 mm and removing off-cuts

Under table guard

25 mm maximum for blades less than 600 mm

At least 225 mm for blades 600 mm and over

Adjustable riving knife to suit saw diameter

12 mm maximum gap

Riving knife 10% thicker than saw plate

WARNING

Minimum diameter of saw blade that may be used in this machine is 360 mm in order to comply with the Woodworking Machines Regulations 1974

Figure 3.7 Circular saw safety requirements

6) A suitable push stick (Figure 3.8) must be provided and kept readily available at all times. It must be used for:
   (a) Feeding material where the cut is 300 mm or less.
   (b) Feeding material over the last 300 mm of the cut.
   (c) Removing cut pieces from between the saw blade and fence.

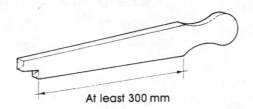

At least 300 mm

Figure 3.8 Push stick

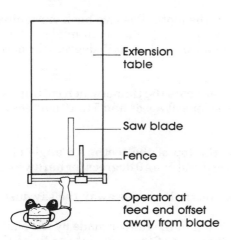

A push block may be used in conjunction with a push stick for cutting short sections.

7) Anyone working at the machine, except the operator, must stand at the delivery end. A full-width table extension must be fitted so that the distance between the nearest part of the saw blade and the end of the table is at least 1200 mm (except in the case of a portable saw bench having a saw blade of 450 mm or less in diameter).

8) The safe working position for the operator is at the feed end offset away from the fence and out of the blade line.

9) It is recommended that operators wear personal protection: ear protection to reduce the risk of hearing loss; dust mask, particularly when cutting hardwood to reduce the risk of respiratory problems.

Extension table

Saw blade

Fence

Operator at feed end offset away from blade

Figure 3.9 Saw operator position

Figure 3.10 Use personal protection when machining

Tooling

The teeth and their terminology for a circular saw blade used for most ripping operations is illustrated in Figure 3.11.

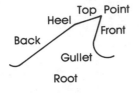

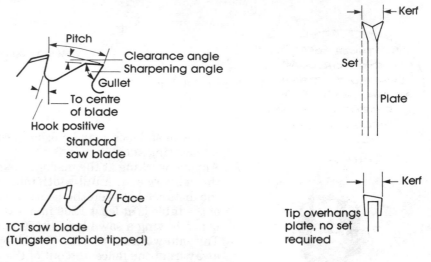

Figure 3.11 Circular rip saw blade terminology

Pitch – is the distance between two teeth.

Hook – is the angle of the front of the tooth. Positive hook is required for ripping. (The teeth incline towards the timber.) An angle of 20 to 25 degrees is normally used for softwoods and 10 to 15 degrees for hardwoods.

Clearance angle – ensures the heel clears the timber when cutting. An angle of 15 degrees is normally used for softwoods and 5 to 10 degrees for hardwoods.

Top bevel – is the angle across the top of the tooth. An angle of 15 degrees is normally used for softwood and 5 to 10 degrees for hardwoods.

Gullet – is the space between two teeth. It carries away the sawdust.

Kerf – is the total width of the saw cut in the timber made by the blade. It equals twice the set plus the thickness of the saw plate or twice the overhang plus the thickness of the saw plate on tungsten carbide tipped saws (TCT).

Set – is the amount each tooth is bent or sprung out to give a clearance on the sawplate. The cutting edge of sprung set blades quickly dull when ripping abrasive timbers. Many sawmills now use tungsten carbide tipped (TCT) saws. These stay sharper much longer and don't require a set as they overhang the sawplate.

Maintenance

Saw blade maintenance

After a period of use, saw blades will start to dull (lose their cutting edge). This will progressively cause a poor finish to the saw cut including burning of both the timber and the blade and possibly cause blade wobble due to overheating. In addition, it will require excessive pressure by the operator to force the timber through the saw.

The sharpening of circular ripsaw blades is normally carried out on a saw sharpening machine or by hand filing. However, neither of these operations are within the scope of this Unit of Competence.

To ensure true running of a saw blade, it should be fitted in the same position on the saw spindle each time it is used. This can be achieved by always mounting the blades on the spindle with the location/driving peg uppermost and, before tightening, pulling the saw blade back onto the peg.

Resin deposits on saw blades should be cleaned off periodically. They can be softened by brushing with an oil/paraffin mixture and scraped off. A wood scraper is preferable as it will avoid scratching the saw blade.

ENSURE MACHINE IS ISOLATED FROM POWER SUPPLY BEFORE UNDERTAKING MAINTENANCE

Machine maintenance

Routine periodic maintenance of the machine will:
- prolong its serviceable life
- ensure all moving parts work freely
- ensure the machine operates safely.

The manufacturer's maintenance schedule supplied with each machine, gives the operator information regarding routine maintenance procedures. The schedule will detail the parts to be lubricated, the location of grease nipples and the type, frequency and amount of grease.

A typical procedure might be:
- Remove all rust spots with fine wire wool.
- Clean off resin deposits and other dirt, using an oil/paraffin mixture and wooden scraper.
- Wipe over entire machine using clean rag.
- Apply a coat of light grade oil to all screws and slides. Excess should be wiped off using a clean rag.
- Clean off grease nipples and apply correct grade and amount of grease using the correct gun. Parts can be rotated manually during this operation.
- Check freeness of all moving parts.

3 Woodworking machining

READ THE INSTRUCTIONS AND COMPLETE THE TASK

——————— **Learning task** ———————

Consult the Woodworking Machine Regulations 1974. (These must be displayed in all areas where woodworking machines are used.) Answer the following questions.

Define a circular sawing machine in accordance with the regulations.

_____

_____

_____

Name the part that covers circular sawing machines.

_____

What paragraph relates to the thickness of a riving knife?

_____

In accordance with the regulations, can a person under 18 years of age who has successfully completed an approved training course, use circular sawing machines without supervision?

_____

TRY TO ANSWER THESE

——————— **Questions for you** ———————

1. Produce sketches to show the difference between deeping and flatting.

2. Name a type of saw blade that is most suitable for ripping abrasive timber.

3. Describe the safe working position that the operator of a circular hand fed saw bench should take.

_____

_____

4. The riving knife fitted to a circular saw must have a maximum clearance between itself and the blade of:
(a) 6 mm
(b) 10 mm
(c) 12 mm
(d) 20 mm

a	b	c	d

5. The guard on a circular saw that covers the top of a saw blade is known as the:
(a) shaw guard
(b) top guard
(c) crown guard
(d) bridge guard

a	b	c	d

6. List **FOUR** general requirements of the Woodworking Machines Regulations 1974.

_____

_____

_____

_____

7. State one piece of information that must be fixed to every circular saw machine.

_____

_____

8. State the purposes of packings to circular saw blades.

_____

_____

9. State **TWO** reasons for using a hardwood mouthpiece.

_____

_____

10. Label the illustration which shows a portion of a circular saw blade.

3
2   4
5
1
6
7

11. State **TWO** reasons for undertaking routine periodic maintenance of woodworking machines.

_____

_____

12. State **TWO** situations where a push stick must be used.

_____

_____

13. List **FIVE** tasks that may be included in the periodic maintenance of a circular saw.

_____

_____

_____

_____

_____

WELL, HOW DID YOU DO?

WORK THROUGH THE SECTION AGAIN IF YOU HAD ANY PROBLEMS

14. Explain why a riving knife thicker than the saw blade should be used.

_____

_____

15. Describe how you would ensure that a saw blade is refitted in exactly the same position after each time it has been taken off for sharpening.

_____

_____

WORD PUZZLE

Solve the clues to complete the word puzzle. All the answers are associated with *'Woodworking Machining'*. The number of letters in each word is shown in brackets e.g. (6) indicates a six-letter word and (4) (3) indicates two words having four and three letters each.

Across

3. Covers top of saw blade (5) (5)
6. To cut out of vertical (5)
7. Sideways projection of saw teeth (3)
9. Not flat (4)
10. Fitted behind saw blade (5) (second word)
11. Fitted to top of saw tooth (3)
13. Sawing with the grain (7)
14. A component being machined (4) (5)

Down

1. Abbreviation for type of saw (3)
2. Used to provide protection (5)
4. Prevents binding (6) (first word)
5. Cutting timber to the required thickness (7)
7. Not required by tipped saws (3)
8. The width of a saw cut (4)
12. Used to rip timber (3)

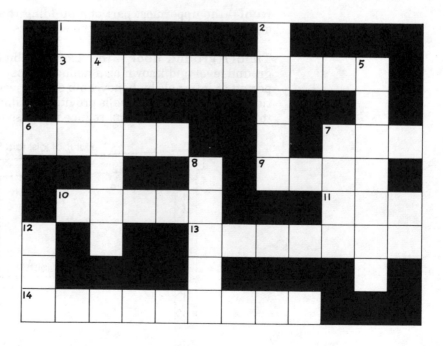

4 Carcassing

READ THIS CHAPTER, WORKING THROUGH THE QUESTIONS AND LEARNING TASKS

In undertaking this chapter you will be required to demonstrate your skill and knowledge of the following carcassing elements:
- Floors, roofs and their finishings.

You will be required practically to:
- Construct an equal pitched roof with hip, valley and gable using trussed rafters and traditional timbers.
- Position and fix fascia board, barge board and soffit.

Floor and flat roof joists

Joist terminology

Floor – the ground or upper levels in a building which provide an acceptable surface for walking, living and working.

Roof – the uppermost part of a building that spans the external walls and provides protection from the elements.

Timber ground floor – the floor of a building nearest the exterior ground level and known as a hollow or suspended floor. Joists are supported at intervals by honeycomb sleeper walls. Air bricks and ventilation gaps in the sleeper walls provide ventilation to the underfloor space to keep the timber dry and reduce the possibility of rot.

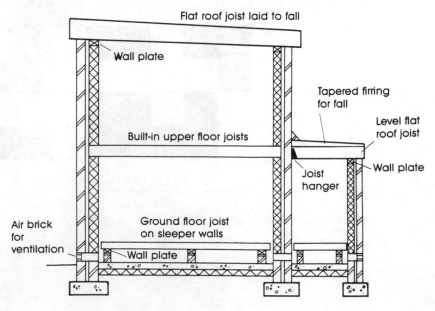

Figure 4.1 Floor and roof joists

Timber upper floors – the floor levels of a building above the ground floor. They are known as suspended floors. Bridging joists span between supports. Binders may be incorporated to reduce span; strutting is used in mid-span to reduce tendency to buckle. Openings in floors are framed using trimming, trimmer and trimmed joists.

Timber flat roofs – any roof having an angle or slope which is less than 10 degrees to the horizontal. They are constructed similar to timber upper floors. The slope on the top surface may be formed by either laying the bridging joist to falls (out of level), or by the use of firrings.

Joist – one of a series of parallel timber beams, used to span the gap between walls and directly support a floor surface, ceiling surface or flat roof surface.

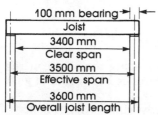

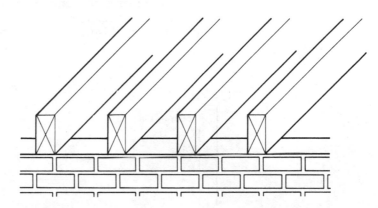

Figure 4.2 Joists

The sectional size of a joist depends on its span, spacing, weight or loading placed upon it and the quality of the timber used. The Building Regulations 1985 Approved Document A (AD:A) Table B contains tables of suitable sectional joist size for use in different situations.

Span – *Clear span* is the distance between joist supports. *Effective span* is the distance between the centres of the joist bearings (see Figure 4.3). The bearing itself is the length of the end of a joist that rests on the support. The overall length of a joist is its clear span plus the length of its end bearings, e.g. a joist with a 3400 mm clear span and 100 mm end bearings will have an effective span of 3500 mm and an overall joist length of 3600 mm.

Joists are commonly laid out to span the shortest distance between the supporting walls of a room or other area. This keeps to a minimum the size of joist required. Once the depth of the joist is determined for the longest span it is normal practice to keep all other joists the same. The shorter span joists will be oversize, but all joist covering and ceiling surfaces will be level.

Spacing – Joist spacing is the distance between the centres of adjacent joists. Commonly called joist centres or c/c (centre to centre). They range between 400 to 600 mm depending on the joist covering material.

Joists should be spaced to accommodate surface dimensions of their covering material. End joists adjacent to walls should be kept 50 mm away from the wall surface, in order to allow an air circulation and prevent dampness being transferred from wall to joist, and thus reduce the risk of rot. In addition this gap helps reduce the transmission of noise at party walls.

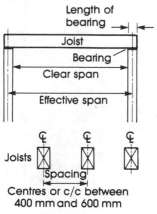

Figure 4.3 Joist span and spacing

61

Unventilated and damp timber is open to an attack of rot (dry rot or wet rot), which lead to a loss of strength and possible collapse. For detailed information on timber rots, their prevention and remedial treatment see *Carpentry and Joinery for Building Craft Students* Books 1 and 2 and/or *Carpentry and Joinery for Advanced Craft Students: Site Practice.*

To determine the number of joists required and their centres for a particular area the following procedure, shown in Figure 4.4, can be used:
- Measure the distance between adjacent walls, say 3150 mm.
- The first and last joist would be positioned 50 mm away from the walls. The centres of 50 mm breadth joists would be 75 mm away from the wall. The total distance between end joists centres would be 3000 mm.
- Divide distance between end joists centres by specified joist spacing say 400 mm. This gives the number of spaces between joists. Where a whole number is not achieved round up to the nearest whole number above. There will always be one more joist than the number of spaces so add one to this figure to determine the number of joists.

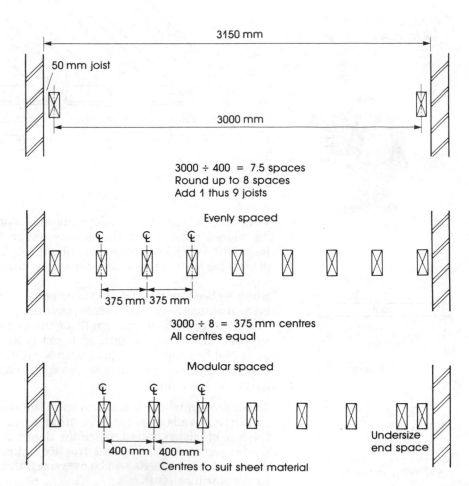

Figure 4.4 Determining number of joists required

- Where T & G boarding is used as a floor covering the joist centres may be spaced out evenly, i.e. divide the distance between end joist centres by the number of spaces.
- Where sheet material is used as a joist covering to form a floor, ceiling or roof surface, the joist centres are normally maintained at a 400 mm or 600 mm module to coincide with sheet sizes. This would leave an undersized spacing between the last two joists.

Joist spacing according to covering material used

Table 4.1 Joist spacing according to covering material used

Covering material	Finished thickness (mm)	Maximum spacing of joists (mm)
Softwood T & G boarding	16	450
Softwood T & G boarding	19	600
Flooring-grade chipboard	18/19	400–450
Flooring-grade chipboard	22	600
Decking plywood	16	400
Decking plywood	18/19	600

Preservative treatment – it is recommended that all timber used for structural purposes is preservative treated before use. Any preservative treated timber cut to size on site will require re-treatment on the freshly cut edges/ends. This can be carried out by applying two brush flood coats of preservative. Timber preservatives prevent rot by poisoning the food supply on which fungi feed and grow. For further information on fungi and timber preservatives see *Carpentry and Joinery for Building Craft Students* Books 1 and 2 and/or *Carpentry and Joinery for Advanced Craft Students: Site Practice*.

Learning task

Determine the number of 50 mm breadth joists required to be spaced at approximately 400 mm centres, between two walls 4350 mm apart.

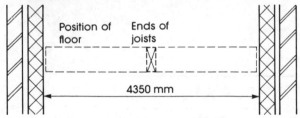

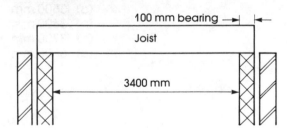

Determine the total amount of timber required in metres run, for all the floor joists. These have a clear span of 3400 mm and a bearing at each end of 100 mm.

If you are unfamiliar with calculations or simply want to 'brush up' before attempting this learning task, refer to *Carpentry and Joinery for Advanced Craft Students: Site Practice*.

TRY TO ANSWER THESE

Questions for you

1. State the purpose of a joist.

_____

_____

2. Why do joists normally span the shortest distance?

_____

_____

3. Define a joist's clear span.

_____

_____

_____

4. The total length of joist having an effective span of 3600 mm and end bearings of 100 mm is:
(a) 3500 mm
(b) 3600 mm
(c) 3700 mm
(d) 3800 mm

a	b	c	d
[ ]	[ ]	[ ]	[ ]

5. A joist spans between two walls 2.8 metres apart and has end bearings of 100 mm, what length of joist is required?

_____

6. Name the regulations that apply to the positioning and fixing of joists.

_____

7. State the reason for treating sawn ends of joists with preservative.

_____

Fixing joists

Section – the breadth and depth of a joist. The strength of a joist varies in direct proportion to changes in its breadth and in proportion to the square of its depth. For example, doubling the breadth of a section doubles its strength.

E.g. a 100 mm × 100 mm joist has double the strength of a 50 mm × 100 mm joist.

Whereas doubling the depth of a section increases its strength by four times.

E.g. a 50 mm × 200 mm joist has four times the strength of a 50 mm × 100 mm joist.

Less material is required for the same strength when the greatest sectional dimension is placed vertically rather than horizontally.

E.g. a 100 mm × 100 mm joist has the same sectional area as a 50 mm × 200 mm joist, but the deeper joist would be twice as strong.

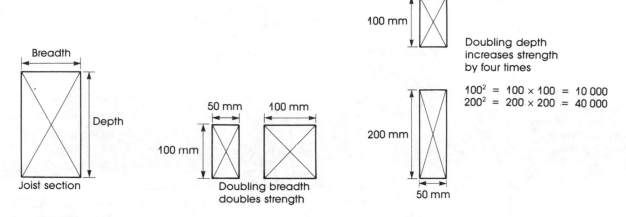

Figure 4.5 Joist section

Therefore joists are normally placed so that the depth is the greatest sectional dimension. Joists of the same sectional size and span would clearly have different strengths if their breadths and depths were reversed. Those with the smaller depth would sag under load, possibly leading to structural collapse (see Figure 4.6). When stating the sectional size of a joist the first measurement given is the breadth and the second the depth.

Regularised timber, as shown in Figure 4.7, is preferred for joists as all timber will be a consistent depth. This aids levelling and ensures a flat fixing surface for joist coverings and ceilings. Joists are regularised to a consistent depth by re-sawing or planing one or both edges. A reduction in size of 3 mm must be allowed for timber up to 150 mm in depth and 5 mm, over this width.

E.g., 50 mm × 150 mm may be regularised to 50 mm × 147 mm and 50 mm × 200 mm may be regularised to 50 mm × 195 mm.

Joist supports – any joists which are not straight should be positioned with their camber or crown (curved edge) upwards. When loaded these joists will tend to straighten out rather than sag further if laid the other way. Joists with edge knots should be positioned with the knots on their upper edge. When loaded the knots will be held in position as the joists sag, rather than fall out, weaken the joist, and possibly lead to structural collapse if laid the other way (see Figure 4.8).

REGULARISED JOISTS HAVE BEEN MACHINED TO A CONSISTENT DEPTH

4 Carcassing

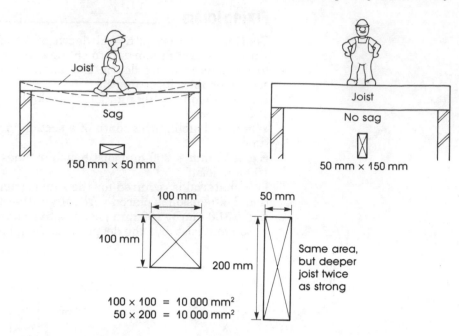

Figure 4.6 Positioning of joist section

50 mm × 200 mm joist
regularised to
50 mm × 195 mm
by machining

Figure 4.7 Regularised joist

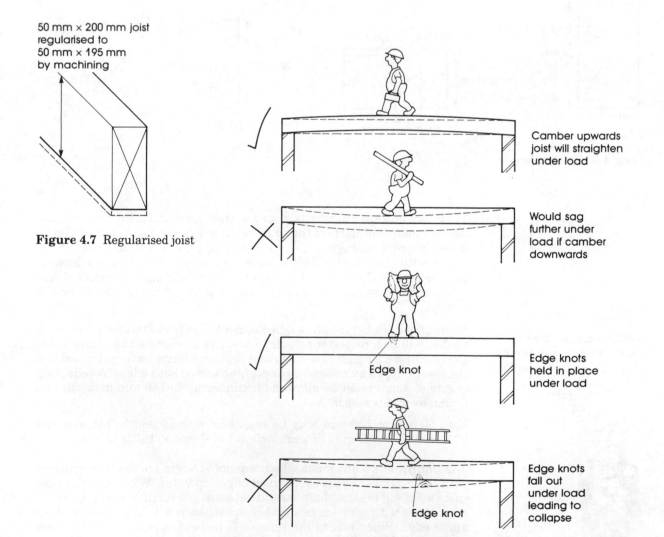

Camber upwards
joist will straighten
under load

Would sag
further under
load if camber
downwards

Edge knots
held in place
under load

Edge knots
fall out
under load
leading to
collapse

Figure 4.8 Positioning of joists with camber or edge knots

Floor and flat roof joists

The ends of joists may be supported:

- by building in
- on hangers
- on wall plates
- on binders

Building in – the inner leaf of a cavity wall (see Figure 4.9). The minimum bearing in a wall is normally 90 mm. (Shorter bearings do not tie in the wall sufficiently and can lead to a crushing of the joist end possibly leading to collapse.) A steel bearing bar may be incorporated into the mortar joint where lightweight blocks are used to reduce the risk of the blocks crumbling. The ends of the joists are often splayed but they must not project into the cavity where they could possibly catch mortar droppings during building, leading to dampness in the joist and rotting. The ends of joists which are in contact with the external wall, should be treated with a timber preservative to protect them from dampness and subsequent rot.

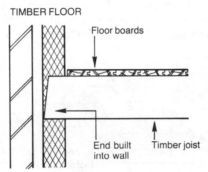

Figure 4.9 Building in a joist

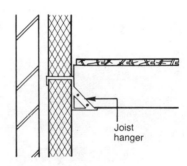

Figure 4.10 Use of joist hanger

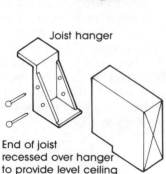

Joist hanger

End of joist recessed over hanger to provide level ceiling

Figure 4.11 Use of joist hanger

Hangers – ends of joists may be supported on galvanised steel joist hangers, which are themselves built into or bear on a wall (see Figure 4.10). Double hangers are available which saddle internal walls to provide a support for joists on both sides. An advantage of this method is that the joist can be positioned independently of the building process. Hangers are useful when forming extensions as they are simply inserted into a raked out mortar joint. The bottom edge or bearing surface of the hanger must be recessed into the joist, as shown in Figure 4.11. This ensures that the top and bottom edges of the joists are flush and also prevent hangers obstructing any ceiling covering. Joists should be secured into the hanger using 32 mm galvanised clout nails in each hole provided.

Wall plates – ends of joists may be supported by a wall plate bedded on the top of a wall. This is normally used for ground floor construction, flat roofs and internal load bearing partitions. The minimum bearing required and thus the minimum width of wall plate is 75 mm. Often joists from either side meet over a wall plate, it is usual to nail them together side by side both overlapping the wall plate by about 300 mm.

The use of wall plates provides a means of securing joists by skew nailing with 75 mm or 100 mm wire nails. In addition, wall plates also spread the loading of a joisted surface evenly over a wide area rather than a point load. Cambered joists may be straightened over a wall plate by partly sawing through and nailing down. Wall plates are not suitable for use in external walls of upper floor construction. This is due to shrinkage movement and the likelihood of rot.

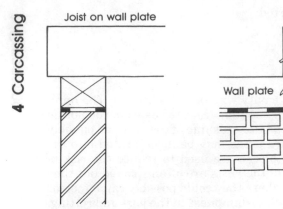

Figure 4.12 Joist supported on a wall plate

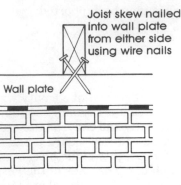

Figure 4.13 Fixing joist to wall plate

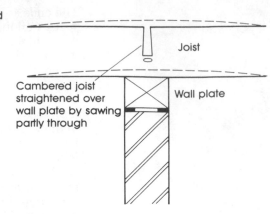

Figure 4.14 Straightening cambered joist at wall plate

Wall plates are jointed by the carpenter using halving joints as shown in Figure 4.15. The plates are bedded and levelled in position by the bricklayer using bedding mortar.

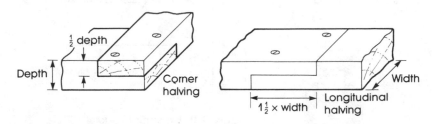

Figure 4.15 Wall plate joint

Binders – are introduced into a structure in order to provide an intermediate support for large span joists. These binders may be of: steel (when they are known as a universal beam (UB)), timber (either of solid section, glue laminated section (glulam) or a plywood box beam) or concrete. Depending on the space available binders may be positioned below the joists, or accommodated partly within the joist depth projecting above or below as required. Where joists are fitted to a steel universal beam, a plywood template may be cut to speed the marking out of the joists and ensure a consistent, accurate fit (see Figure 4.17).

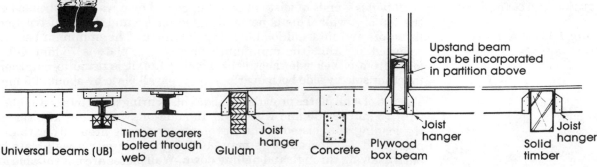

Figure 4.16 Binders

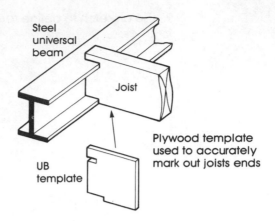

Figure 4.17 Marking and cutting a joist to fit a universal beam

Restraint straps – with modern lightweight structures, walls and joisted areas require positive tying together for strength, to ensure wall stability. Galvanised mild steel restraint straps should be used at not more than 2 metre intervals for joists parallel to the wall, at right angles to the wall and those on wall plates.

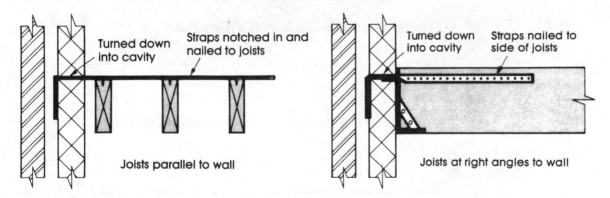

Figure 4.18 Restraint straps

Questions for you

8. Two pieces of timber are of the same sectional area, one is 100 mm × 100 mm and the other is 50 mm × 200 mm.
(a) Which is best for use as a joist?
(b) State why.

9. Use a sketch to define regularised timber.

10. State why joists should not project into wall cavities.

_____

_____

11. State the minimum joist bearing when:
(a) building in
(b) on wall plates.

_____

_____

12. State why regularised joists are preferred.

_____

_____

13. State a reason for recessing joists to receive joist hangers.

_____

_____

14. State the total metres run of timber required for six joists each spanning 3.6 metres and being supported by joist hangers.

_____

_____

15. State the purpose of binders.

_____

_____

16. State the purpose of restraint straps.

_____

17. At what centres should restraint straps be fixed?

_____

18. State the purpose of a template when cutting joists into a steel binder.

_____

_____

19. Produce sketches to illustrate the following:
(a) a joist hanger

(b) a binder

(c) a wall plate lengthening (longitudinal) joint

(d) a restraint strap

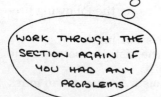

Joist restraint

Strutting – where deep joists exceed a span of 2 metres, they tend to buckle and/or sag under load, unless restrained by strutting. Joists spanning between 2 and 3.6 metres should be restrained by strutting at their mid-span; larger span joists should be restrained at about 1.8 metre intervals. There are three main types of strutting in use:
- Galvanised steel strutting
- Solid timber strutting
- Herring-bone timber strutting

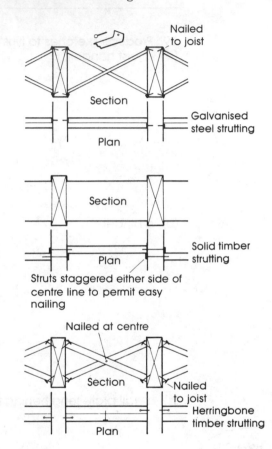

Figure 4.19 Strutting to joists

Galvanised steel strutting has a disadvantage in that the depth and centres of the joist must be specified when ordering; different depths and spacings will require different sized struts.

Solid strutting is quick to install but is considered inferior as it tends to loosen and become ineffective when joists shrink.

Herring-bone timber strutting is considered the most effective as it actually tightens when joists shrink. However, it takes longer to install and thus is more expensive in terms of labour costs.

Herring-bone timber struts can be marked out using the following procedure shown in Figure 4.20.
- Mark across the joists the centre line of the strutting.
- Mark a second line across the joist so that the distance between the lines is 10 mm less than the depth of the joist.
- Place the length of strutting on top of the joists as shown and mark underneath against the joists at A and B.

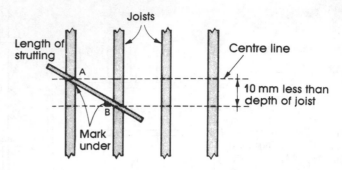

Figure 4.20 Marking out strutting

- Cut two struts to these marks. If all joists are spaced evenly, all the strutting will be the same size and can be cut using the first one as a template. If not, each set of struts will have to be marked individually.
- Fix struts on either side of the centre line using wire nails, one in the top and bottom of each strut and one through the centre.

Whichever method of strutting is used, care should be taken to ensure that they are clear of the tops and bottoms of the joists, otherwise they may subsequently distort the joist covering or ceiling surface.

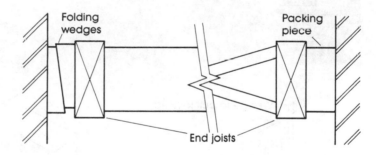

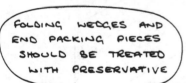

FOLDING WEDGES AND END PACKING PIECES SHOULD BE TREATED WITH PRESERVATIVE

Figure 4.21 Strutting tightened using a packing piece and folding wedges

Again, whichever method of strutting is used, the gaps between the end joists and the walls will require packing and wedging to complete the system. Care must be taken not to overtighten the folding wedges as it is possible to dislodge the blockwork.

Trimming – where openings are required in joisted areas or where projections occur in supporting walls, joists must be framed or trimmed around them (see Figure 4.22). Members used for trimming each have their own function and are named accordingly.

Bridging joist – a joist spanning from support to support, also known as a common joist.

Trimmed joist – a bridging joist that has been cut short (trimmed) to form an opening in the floor.

Trimmer joist – a joist placed at right angles to the bridging joist, in order to support the cut ends of the trimmed joists.

Trimming joist – a joist with a span the same as the bridging joist, but supporting the end of a trimmer joist.

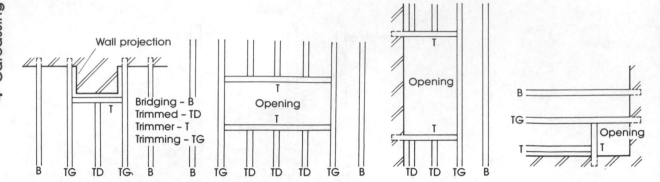

Figure 4.22 Trimming openings

As both the trimmer and the trimming joists take a greater load, they are usually 25 mm thicker in breadth than the bridging joists. For example, use 75 mm × 200 mm trimmer and trimming joists with 50 mm × 200 mm bridging joists.

The Building Regulations 1985 Approved Document J (AD:J) Heat Producing Appliances restrict the positioning and trimming of timber near sources of heat. Full details of the requirements when trimming in such locations are contained in *Carpentry and Joinery For Advanced Craft Students: Site Practice*.

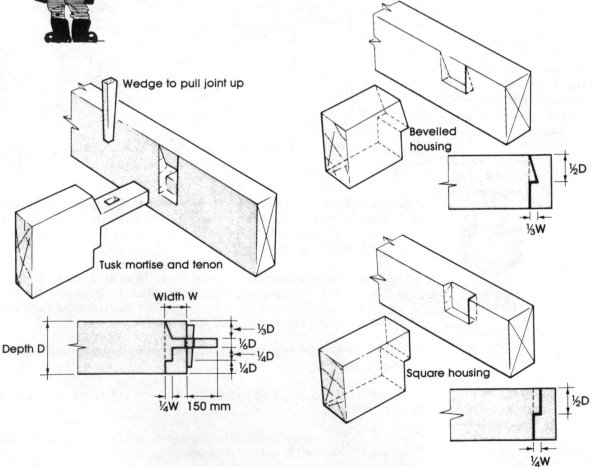

Figure 4.23 Traditional trimming joists

Trimming joints – Traditionally, tusk mortise and tenon joints were used between the trimmer and trimming joists, while housing joints were used between the trimmed joists and the trimmer. Once wedged the tusk mortise and tenon joint requires no further fixing. The housing joints will require securing with 100 mm wire nails. The proportions of these joints must be followed. They are based on the fact that there are neutral stress areas in joists (see Figure 4.24), if any cutting is restricted mainly to this area then the reduction in the joist strength will be kept to a minimum. Joist hangers which are a quicker modern alternative to the traditional joints are now used almost exclusively. As these hangers are made from thin galvanised steel, they do not require recessing in as do the thicker wall hangers but they must be securely nailed in each hole provided with 32 mm galvanised clout nails.

Joints cut in shaded areas will cause the minimum reduction in strength

Figure 4.24 Neutral stress areas

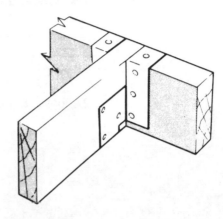

Figure 4.25 Trimming using a joist hanger

TRY TO ANSWER THESE

Questions for you

20. State the purpose of strutting joists.

_____

_____

21. What is the disadvantage of solid strutting?

_____

_____

22. Name the type of nail used to fix timber herringbone strutting.

_____

23. State why strutting should be kept clear of the joists top and bottom edges.

_____

_____

24. State the purpose of trimming joists.

_____

_____

25. Name the regulations which apply to the trimming of joists near to sources of heat.

_____

_____

26. What type of nails are used for fixing a thin galvanised steel joist hanger used to connect a trimmed joist to a trimmer?

_____

_____

27. Use a sketch to define the neutral stress areas of a joist.

WELL, HOW DID YOU DO?

WORK THROUGH THE SECTION AGAIN IF YOU HAD ANY PROBLEMS

28. Produce a sketch to illustrate the proportions of a tusk mortise and tenon joint.

Positioning joists

Storey rod

Wall plate

Lintel

Window sill

Floor

Lintel

Brick courses

Window sill

DPC oversite

Figure 4.26 Storey rod

Layout of joists – the positioning of joists is a fairly simple operation. The first task is to establish their vertical position in the building. (For joists built-in or on wall plates the vertical position will have been fixed by the bricklayer.) Vertical positioning in a building is commonly achieved by either the use of a storey rod, shown in Figure 4.26, which is marked out before work commences and fixed in one corner, or by datum marks/lines which are positioned at a convenient height around the walls of a building and indicated by an arrow and horizontal line as shown in Figure 4.27. A set measurement up from the datum will establish the position of the joists.

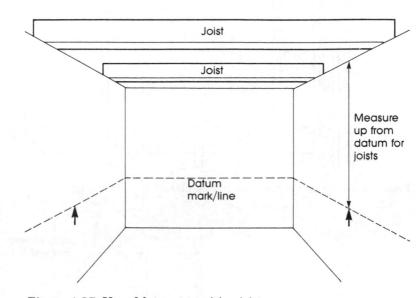

Joist

Joist

Measure up from datum for joists

Datum mark/line

Figure 4.27 Use of datum to position joists

The outside bridging joists are placed in position first, leaving a 50 mm gap between them and the wall. The other joists are then spaced out to the required centres in the remaining area.

However, when openings for fireplaces and stairwells, etc., are required in the joisted area the layout of the joists is governed by these openings. The trimming and outside bridging joists are the first to be positioned, once again leaving a 50 mm gap between all joists and the walls. The other joists are then spaced out to the required centres in the remaining areas as shown in Figure 4.28.

Double joists are required where blockwork partition walls are to be built on a joisted area. These double joists are either nailed or bolted together (depending on specification), and positioned under the intended wall to take the additional load. When laying out a joisted area, double joists are positioned along with the trimming and end bridging joists, before the other joists are spaced.

In order to span the shortest direction it is sometimes necessary to change the direction of joists in a particular joisted area. This is done over a load-bearing wall where the bridging joists from one area are allowed to overhang by 50 mm, the end bridging joist in the other area is simply nailed to the overhanging ends (see Figure 4.30).

Levelling joists – After positioning, the joists should be checked for line and level. End joists are set using a spirit level; intermediate joists are

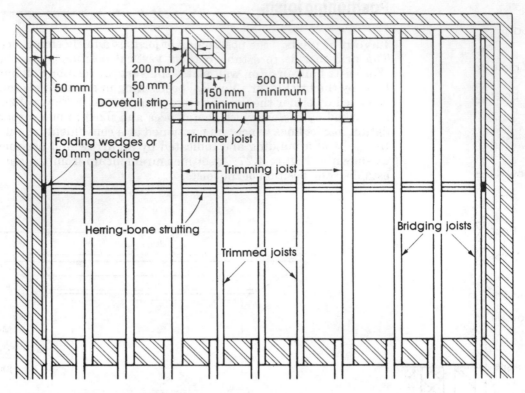

Figure 4.28 Layout of floor around fireplace

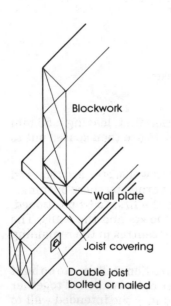

Figure 4.29 Double joists required to support blockwork partition above

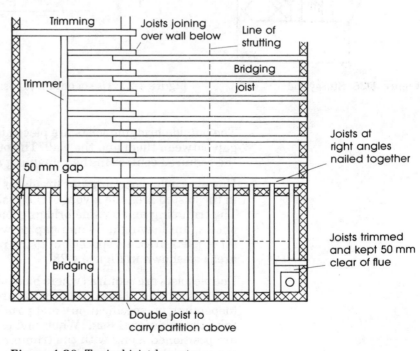

Figure 4.30 Typical joist layout

lined through with a straight edge and spirit level (see Figure 4.31). Where the brickwork or blockwork course has been finished to a level line by the bricklayer or where wall plates are used and have been accurately bedded level, and where regularised joists have been used, the bearings of the joist should not require any adjustment to bring

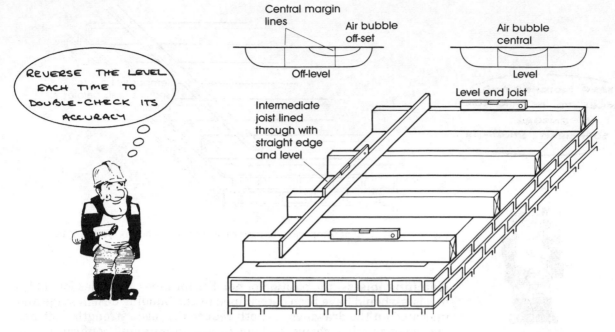

Figure 4.31 Levelling joists

them into line and level. However, minor adjustments may be required as shown in Figure 4.32. Joists may be housed into or packed off wall plates. Where packings are required for built-in joists, these should be slate or other durable material. Do not use timber packings as these may shrink and work loose and in any case are susceptible to rot. Joists may be recessed, to lower their bearing, providing the reduced joist depth is still sufficient for its span.

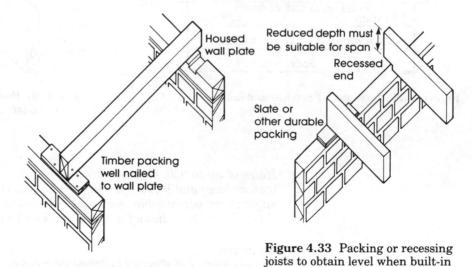

Figure 4.33 Packing or recessing joists to obtain level when built-in

Figure 4.32 Packing or housing joists to obtain level on wall plate

Figure 4.34 shows temporary battens which can be nailed across the top of the joists to ensure that their spacing remains constant before and during their 'building in'. Joists fixed to wall plates can be skew nailed to them using 75 mm or 100 mm wire nails.

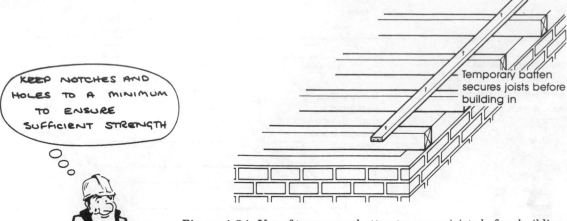

Figure 4.34 Use of temporary batten to secure joists before building in

Notching joists – the position of notches for pipes and holes for cables in joists, should have been determined at the building design stage and indicated on the drawings, as both reduce the joists strength. Notches and holes in joists should be kept to a minimum and conform to the following:

Notches on the joist's top edge of up to 0.125 of the joist's depth located between 0.07 and 0.25 of the span from either support are permissible.

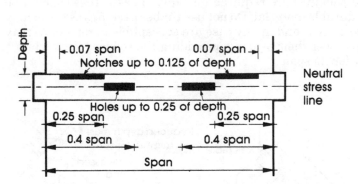

Figure 4.35 Positions for notches and holes

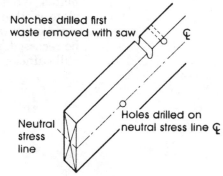

Figure 4.36 Positioning of notches and holes to accommodate services

Holes of up to 0.25 of the joist's depth drilled on the neutral stress line (centre line) and located between 0.25 and 0.4 of the span from either support are permissible. Adjacent holes should be separated by at least three times their diameter measured centre to centre.

Example
The position and sizes for notches and holes in a 200 mm depth joist spanning 4000 mm are:
Notches – between 280 mm and 1000 mm in from each end of the joist and up to 25 mm deep.
Holes – between 1000 mm and 1600 mm in from each end of the joist and up to 50 mm diameter.

Excessive notching and drilling of holes outside the permissible limits will seriously weaken the joist and may lead to structural failure.

READ THE INSTRUCTIONS
AND COMPLETE
THE TASK

Learning task

The plan of the building at upper floor joist bearing level is shown.
Internal walls are to receive a wall plate.
Joists are to be built into the external walls.
The flue is 500 mm square.
Double joists are required where partitions are to be built on the floor.

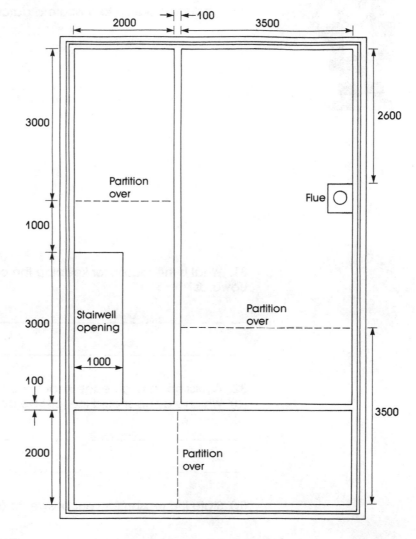

Tasks

1. Determine and indicate on the drawing the position of all joists.
2. Name on the drawing all joists.
3. Indicate on the drawing any strutting required.
4. Produce a list of all materials required to complete the joist layout.

_____

_____

_____

_____

_____

29. State the purpose of a datum.

_____

_____

30. Produce a sketch to illustrate a datum mark/line.

31. What is the reason for keeping the camber or crown of a joist upwards?

_____

_____

32. A joist has a large edge knot towards the centre of its span.
(a) Which way up should the joist be positioned?

_____

_____

(b) State the reason for your answer to (a).

_____

_____

33. State the reason why joists adjacent to walls are kept 50 mm away.

_____

_____

34. State the purpose of a trimmer joist used when forming openings.

_____

_____

35. State the purpose of notching and boring holes in joists.

_____

_____

36. Why are temporary battens sometimes fixed across the tops of joists?

_____

_____

37. State the maximum diameter hole that can be bored in a 200 mm deep joist.

_____

38. Produce a sketch to show how a notch in the top of a joist could be formed to receive a 25 mm diameter pipe.

WELL, HOW DID YOU DO?

WORK THROUGH THE SECTION AGAIN IF YOU HAD ANY PROBLEMS

39. State the likely effect of excessive or wrongly placed notching to joists.

_____

_____

40. State why timber should not be used when packing joists to line in an external wall.

_____

_____

4 Carcassing

COMPLETE THE WORD SQUARE

WORD-SQUARE SEARCH

Hidden in the word square are the following 20 words associated with '*Joists*'. You may find the words written forwards, backwards, up, down or diagonally.

Floor	Binder
Roof	Restraint
Wallplate	Herringbone
Span	Notching
Pitch	Packing
Hanger	Crown
Strutting	Datum
Preservative	Trimmer
Regularised	Trimmed
Building in	Trimming

Draw a ring around the words, or line in using a highlight pen thus:

EXAMPLE

EXAMPLE

P	L	A	N	F	O	R	S	T	R	I	M	M	E	D	O	C	S
R	U	S	O	L	I	P	H	E	A	D	S	R	R	E	W	O	T
E	R	T	T	A	A	M	F	D	N	D	H	O	M	G	P	H	R
S	I	C	C	N	D	D	E	R	L	C	P	F	N	M	E	E	U
E	A	R	H	O	Y	A	N	E	T	E	O	I	D	U	H	R	T
R	U	O	I	N	G	O	T	G	G	O	M	S	E	T	E	R	T
V	A	W	N	E	F	L	O	O	R	M	D	N	S	R	L	I	I
A	N	N	G	P	T	S	S	L	I	L	S	A	I	I	M	N	N
T	I	T	O	S	N	S	E	R	I	P	O	R	R	M	E	G	G
I	G	C	O	C	I	P	T	T	R	E	S	T	A	M	T	B	N
V	N	O	R	I	A	O	A	I	M	L	H	O	L	E	S	O	I
E	I	N	E	R	R	G	L	O	U	O	A	E	U	R	T	N	W
R	D	S	P	E	T	D	P	N	T	S	N	B	G	N	P	E	A
O	L	T	V	D	S	S	L	S	A	E	G	O	E	C	C	E	P
L	I	R	C	N	E	P	L	E	D	S	E	A	R	I	O	I	D
K	U	A	T	I	R	L	A	T	T	E	R	R	O	D	T	N	V
F	B	C	T	B	S	B	W	L	A	D	E	D	E	C	S	I	E
P	A	C	K	I	N	G	O	C	A	T	S	R	H	G	D	E	L

Joist coverings

Joist coverings are often termed decking; the main materials in common use for this are:

- Timber floor boards mainly PTG (planed, tongued and grooved) but square-edged boarding may be used for roofing.
- Flooring grade particle board, mainly tongued and grooved or square-edged chipboard, but wafer or flake board is also used.
- Flooring grade plywood either tongued and grooved or square-edged.

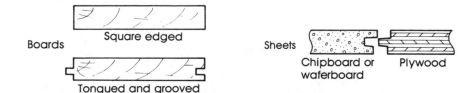

Boards — Square edged

Tongued and grooved

Sheets — Chipboard or waferboard — Plywood

Figure 4.37 Joist coverings

Floorboarding is normally carried out after timber carcassing and preferably also after the window glazing and roof tiling is complete so that it is not exposed to the weather. Boarding or decking to flat roofs should be carried out just before they are to be waterproofed. Chipboard roof sheets are available pre-covered with a layer of felt to provide some measure of initial protection.

Softwood flooring

Softwood flooring usually consists of ex 25 mm × 150 mm tongued and grooved boarding.

A standard floorboard section has the tongue and groove offset away from the board's face. This identifies the upper face and also provides an increased wearing surface before exposing the tongue and groove. Boards can be fixed either by floor brads nailed through the surface of the boards and punched in, or by lost-head nails secret-fixed through the tongue as shown in Figure 4.38. Nails should be approximately 2½ times the thickness of the floorboard in length. Figure 4.39 shows square-butted or splayed heading joints which are introduced as required to utilise offcuts of board and avoid wastage. Splayed heading joints are preferred as there is less risk of the board end splitting. Heading joints should be staggered evenly throughout the floor for strength; these should never be placed next to each other, as the joists and covering would not be tied together properly.

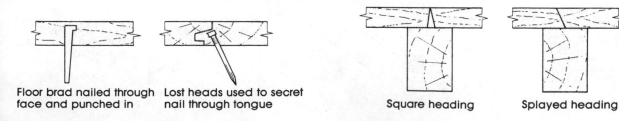

Floor brad nailed through face and punched in   Lost heads used to secret nail through tongue

Square heading   Splayed heading

Figure 4.38 Fixing softwood flooring   **Figure 4.39** Heading joints for softwood flooring

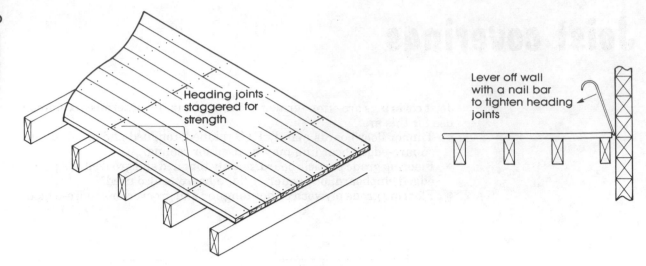

Figure 4.40 Positioning of heading joints

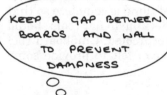

Surface fixing

Boards are laid at right angles to the joists. The first board should be fixed at least 10 mm away from the outside wall. This gap which is later covered by the skirting, helps to prevent dampness being absorbed through direct wall contact. In addition, the gap also allows the covering material to expand without either causing pressure on the wall or a bulging of the floor surface. The remainder of the boards are laid four to six at a time, cramped up with floorboard cramps (see Figure 4.41) and surface nailed to the joists. The final nailing of a floor is often termed 'bumping'. This should be followed by punching the nail head just below the surface. Boards up to 100 mm in width require one nail to each joist while boards over this require two nails.

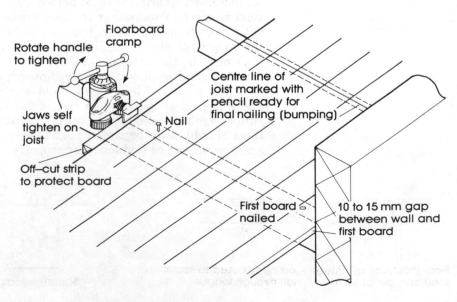

Figure 4.41 Use of floorboard cramp

Figure 4.42 shows two alternatives to the use of floorboard cramps are folding or wedging, although neither of these is as quick or efficient. Folding a floor entails fixing two boards spaced apart 10 mm less than the width of five boards. The five boards can then be placed with their tongues and grooves engaged. A short board is laid across the centre and 'jumped on' to press the boards in position. This process is then repeated across the rest of the floor. Alternatively, the boards may be cramped, four to six at a time using dogs and wedges.

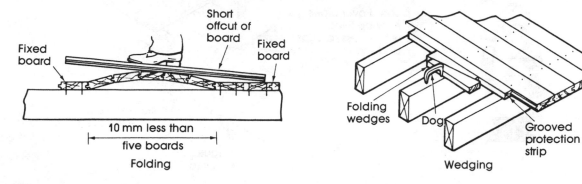

Figure 4.42 Tightening floorboards

Secret fixing

Secret-fixed boards must be laid and tightened individually and cramping is therefore not practical. Figure 4.43 shows how they may be tightened by levering them forward with a firmer chisel driven into the top of the joist, or with the aid of a floorboard nailer. This tightens the boards and drives the nail when the plunger is struck with a hard mallet.

Secret fixing is normally only used on high class work or hardwood flooring, as the increased laying time makes it considerably more expensive.

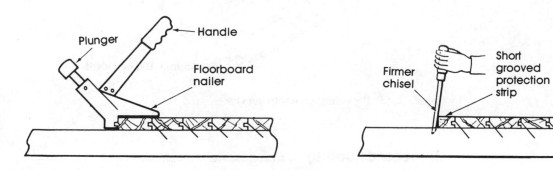

Figure 4.43 Tightening secret-fixed floorboards

Services

Where services such as water and gas pipes or electric cables are run within the floor, there is a danger of driving nails into them. They should be marked on laying in chalk or pencil 'PIPES NO FIXING', so that on nailing the danger area is kept clear. Alternatively, the floorboards over services can be fixed with recessed cups and screws to permit easy

Figure 4.44 Marking position of services

removal for subsequent access, and also to provide easy recognition of location.

Access traps, Figure 4.45, may be required in a floor over areas where water stop cocks or electrical junction boxes are located. Again these can be fixed with recessed cups and screws to permit easy removal.

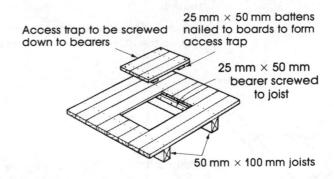

Figure 4.45 Providing access to services

Chipboard flooring

This is now being increasingly used for domestic flooring. Flooring grade chipboard is available with square edges in 1220 mm × 2440 mm sheets, and with tongued and grooved edges in 600 mm × 2440 mm sheets. Square-edged sheets are normally laid with their long edges over a joist. Noggins must be fixed between the joists to support the short ends. Tongued and grooved sheets are usually laid with their long edges at right angles to the joists and their short edges joining over the joist. Both types require noggins between the joists where the sheet abuts a wall. Joists should be spaced to accommodate the dimensions of the sheet flooring.

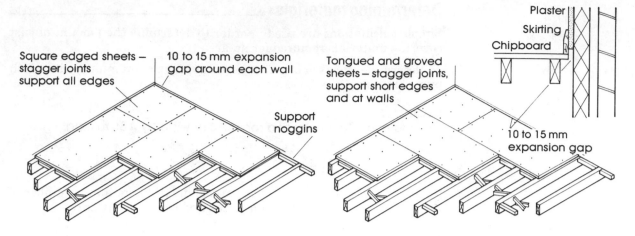

Figure 4.46 Layout of chipboard floors

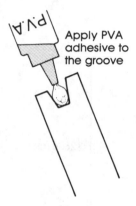

Figure 4.47 Gluing joints in chipboard flooring

Fixing

Sheets are laid staggered and fixed at 200 mm to 300 mm centres with 50 mm lost-head nails or, for additional strength, annular ring shanked or serrated nails. A gap of 10 mm must be left along each wall to allow for expansion and prevent absorbtion of dampness from the wall. Manufacturers of chipboard often recommend the gluing of the tongues and grooves with a PVA adhesive to prevent joint movement and stiffen the floor.

For protection it is recommended that the floor is covered with building paper after laying and that this is left in position until the building is occupied.

Plywood flooring is laid using the same procedures as chipboard flooring.

Flat roof decking

The choice of materials and method of laying decking can be likened to floors with the exception that where timber boards are used they should be laid either with, or at a diagonal to, the fall of the roof's surface. Cupping or distortion of the boards can lead to pools of water being trapped in hollows formed on the roof's surface, where boards are laid at right angles to the fall.

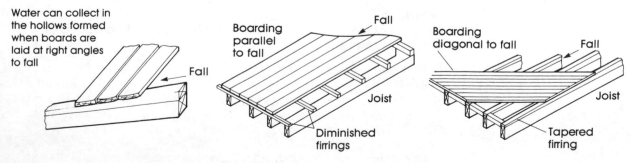

Figure 4.48 Timber boards for flat roof decking

Determining materials

Simple calculations are used in order to determine the amount of joist covering materials required for an area.

To determine the area of a simple rectangular room multiply its width by its length.

Example
Calculate the floor area of a room 3.6 m wide by 4.85 m long.

Area of floor $= 3.6 \times 4.85$
$= 17.46\,m^2$

To determine more complex floor areas, divide them into a number of rectangles or other recognisable areas and solve each in turn.

Example
Calculate the floor area of the room shown in Figure 4.49. This can be divided into two rectangles, A & B, each being solved separately then added together. (As an area in square metres, m², is required change all dimensions to metres before starting.)

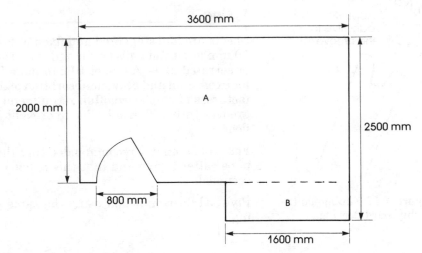

Figure 4.49

Area of A $= 2 \times 3.6$
$= 7.2\,m^2$

Area of B $= 0.5 \times 1.6$
$= 0.8\,m^2$

Area of floor $= A + B$
$= 7.2 + 0.8$
$= 8\,m^2$

Example
The area of the room shown in Figure 4.50 is equal to area A plus area B minus area C.

Area A
(Trapezium) $= \dfrac{9 + 10.5}{2} \times 6.75$
$= 65.813\,m^2$

Area B $= 0.75 \times 5.5$
$= 4.125\,m^2$

Area C $= 0.9 \times 3$
$= 2.7\,m^2$

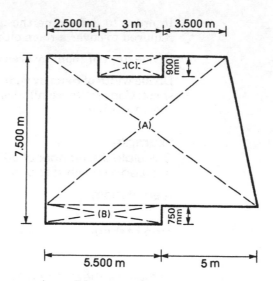

Figure 4.50

Total area of floor = A + B − C
= 65.813 + 4.125 − 2.7
= 67.238 m²

In order to determine the metres run of floorboards required to cover a room, the floor area is divided by the board's covering width.

Example
Calculate the metres run of floorboards required to cover a floor area of 4.65 m², if the floorboards have a covering width of 137 mm. (Change 137 mm to metres before starting by moving its imaginary point behind the 7 three places forward to become 0.137 m. This is because all the units in a calculation must be the same.)

Metres run required = Area ÷ Width of board
= 4.65 ÷ 0.137
= 33.94 m
say 34 m run.

It is standard practice to order an additional amount of flooring to allow for cutting and wastage. This is often between 10% and 15%.

To calculate the metres run of floor boarding required plus an additional percentage, turn the percentage into a decimal,

e.g. 5% = 0.05   10% = 0.1   25% = 0.25

Place a one in front of the point (to include original amount) and use this number to multiply the original amount e.g. for 5% increase use 1.05, for 10% increase use 1.1, for 25% increase use 1.25. (See also p. 131.)

Example
If 34 m run of floorboarding is required to cover an area, calculate the amount to be ordered including an additional 12% for cutting and wastage. (For 12% increase multiply by 1.12.)

Amount to be ordered = 34 × 1.12
= 38.08
say 38 m run.

In order to determine the number of sheets of plywood or chipboard required to cover a room either:

Divide area of room by area of sheet, or

Divide width of room by width of sheet, divide length of room by length of sheet. Convert these numbers to the nearest whole or half and multiply them together.

Example

Calculate the number of 600 mm × 2400 mm chipboard sheets required to cover a floor area of 2.05 m × 3.6 m.

Area of room	= 2.05 × 3.6
	= 7.38 m²
Area of sheet	= 0.6 × 2.4
	= 1.44 m²

$$\text{Number of sheets required} = \frac{\text{Area of room}}{\text{Area of sheet}}$$
$$= 7.38 \div 1.44$$
$$= 5.125$$
$$\text{say 6 sheets}$$

or alternatively,

Number of sheet widths in room width	= 2.05 ÷ 0.6
	= 3.417
	say 3.5
Number of sheet lengths in room length	= 3.6 ÷ 2.4
	= 1.5
Total number of sheets	= 3.5 × 1.5
	= 5.25
	say 6 sheets.

READ THE INSTRUCTIONS AND COMPLETE THE TASK

Learning task

The bungalow shown below is to have a timber suspended hollow ground floor to all rooms except the garage. The overall internal measurements are 10 950 mm × 6650 mm, the garage is 2750 mm × 4550 mm.

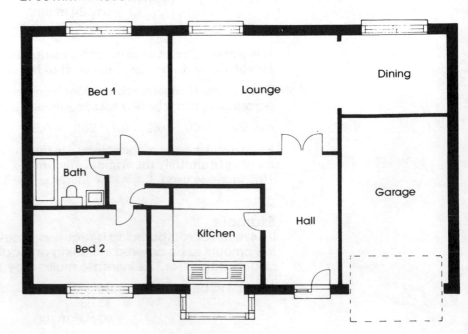

Determine the overall floor area in square metres (including the garage).

_____

_____

_____

_____

Determine the required area of joist covering in metres square.

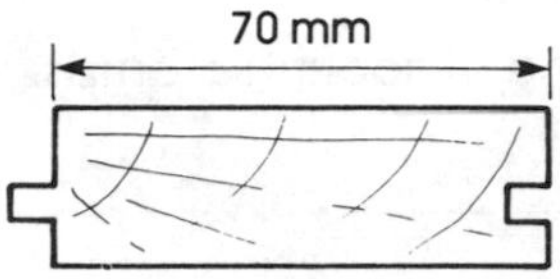

_____

_____

_____

_____

70 mm

Calculate the amount of T & G boarding required in metres run; allow 15% extra as a cutting allowance.

_____

_____

_____

_____

_____ **Questions for you** _____

TRY TO ANSWER THESE

41. Produce a sketch to show the section of a tongued and grooved floorboard.

42. State the purpose of heading joints in timber boarded floor surfaces and explain why they should be staggered.

_____

_____

43. State a reason why an access trap may be required in joist covering.

_____

_____

44. State the reason why a gap is left between joist coverings and adjacent walls.

_____

_____

45. Name a nail and state its length which is suitable for the surface fixing of a 20 mm finished thickness floorboard.

_____

_____

46. Explain **ONE** method which can be used to cramp up tongued and grooved floorboards in the absence of flooring cramps.

_____

_____

47. Explain the purpose of noggins when using sheet joist coverings.

_____

_____

48. Explain the purpose of gluing the tongues and grooves of sheet joist coverings.

_____

_____

49. Name one nail suitable for fixing sheet joist coverings.

_____

50. Produce a sketch to show what is meant by secret fixing when applied to tongued and grooved floorboards.

WELL, HOW DID YOU DO?

WORK THROUGH THE SECTION AGAIN IF YOU HAD ANY PROBLEMS

Floor and flat roof joists

WORD-SQUARE SEARCH

Hidden in the word square are the following 20 words associated with '*Fixing joist coverings*'. You may find the words written forwards, backwards, up, down or diagonally.

Fixing	Secret
Joist	Softwood
Coverings	Tongue and groove
Floor	Square edge
Ground	Chipboard
Upper	Waferboard
Roof	Plywood
Timber	Noggins
Boarding	Cramp
Services	Bumping

Draw a ring around the words, or line in using a highlight pen thus:

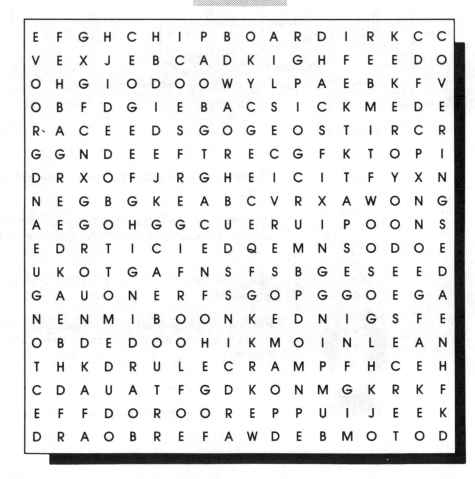

Timber pitched roofs

Roof terminology

Roof – the uppermost part of a building that spans the external walls and provides protection from the elements. Roofs may be classified as either pitched or flat and further variously named according to their shape.

Pitched roof – any roof having a sloping surface in excess of 10 degrees pitch. Those with a single sloping surface are known as mono pitch and those with two opposing sloping surfaces are known as double pitched.

Gable roof – a double pitched roof with one or more gable ends.

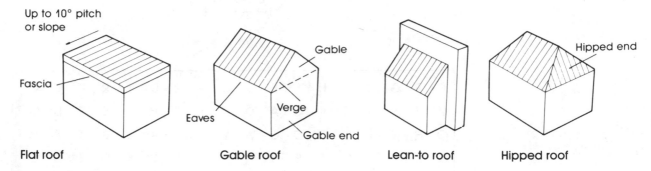

Figure 4.51 Types of roof

Gable – the triangular portion of the end wall of the building with a pitched roof.

Hipped roof – a double pitched roof where the roof slope is returned around the shorter sides of the building to form a sloping triangular end.

Flat roof – any roof having a pitch or slope of up to 10 degrees to the horizontal.

Pitch – the angle of a roof's inclination to the horizontal, or the ratio of rise to span, e.g. a one third pitch roof with a span of 6 metres will rise 2 metres.

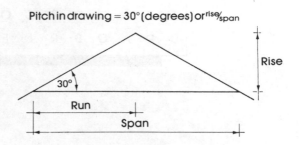

Figure 4.52 Roof pitch

Verge – the termination or edge of a pitched roof at the gable end or a flat roof at the sloping edge. Both often overhang the wall and are finished with a barge board and soffit.

Eaves – the lowest part of a pitched roof slope where the ends of the rafters terminate, or the level edge of a flat roof. Both usually overhang the wall and are finished with a fascia board soffit.

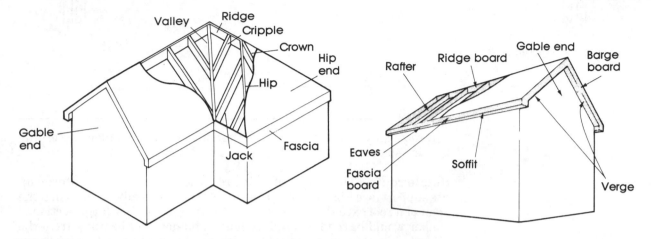

Figure 4.53 Roof terminology

Valley – the intersection of two pitched roof surfaces at an internal corner.

Construction terminology

Timber pitched roofs may be divided into two broad but distinct categories:
- **Traditional framed cut roofs** – entirely constructed in situ from loose, sawn timber sections and utilising simple jointing methods.
- **Prefabricated trussed rafters** – normally manufactured in factory conditions from prepared timber butt-jointed and secured using nail plates.

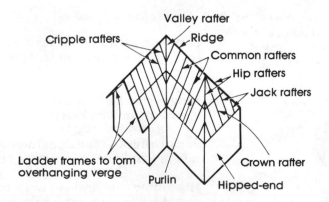

Figure 4.54 Terminology for traditional framed cut roof

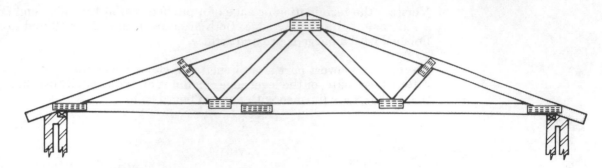

Figure 4.55 Trussed rafter

Cut roofs

Cut roofs may be constructed as either single or double roofs, according to their span.

Single roofs – The rafters of single roofs do not require any intermediate support (see Figure 4.56). They are not economically viable when the span of a roof exceeds about 5.5 m. This is because very large sectioned timber would have to be used. A central binder may be hung from the ridge to bind together and prevent any sagging when ceiling joists are used in a close coupled single roof.

Double roofs – The rafters of double roofs are of such a length that they require an intermediate support (see Figure 4.57). This is normally given by purlins to support the rafters in mid span.

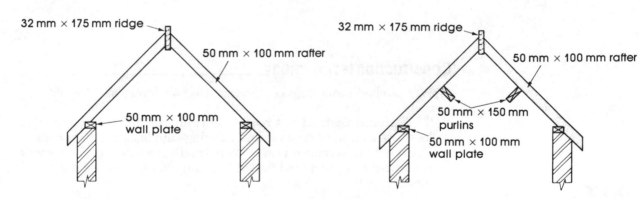

Figure 4.56 Section through a single roof

Figure 4.57 Section through a double roof

Common rafters – the main loadbearing timbers in a roof, which are cut to fit the ridge and birdsmouthed over the wall plate (see Figure 4.58).

Ridge – the backbone of the roof which provides a fixing point for the tops of the rafters, keeping them in line.

Jack rafters – span from the wall plate to the hip rafter, like common rafters that have had their tops shortened.

Hip rafter – used where two sloping roof surfaces meet at an angle. It provides a fixing point for the jack rafters and transfers their loads to the wall.

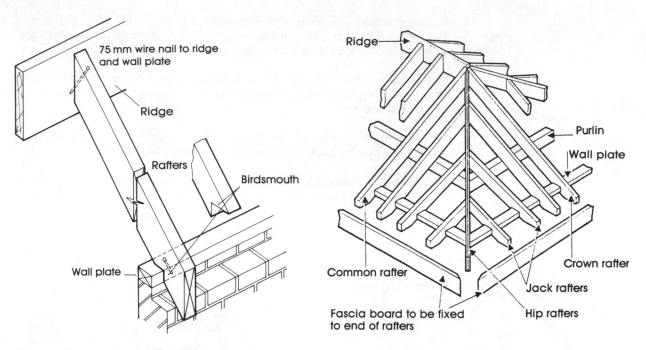

Figure 4.58 Fixing a common rafter

Figure 4.59 Hip-end detail

Cripple rafters – span from the ridge to the valley, like common rafters that have had their feet shortened (the reverse of jack rafters).

Valley rafter – like the hip rafter but forming an internal angle.

Purlin – a beam that provides support for the rafters in their mid-span.

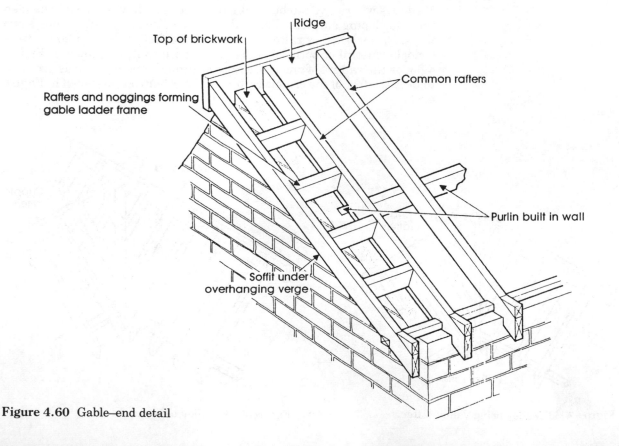

Figure 4.60 Gable–end detail

Ladder frame – This is also known as a gable ladder and is fixed to the last common rafter to form the overhanging verge on a gable roof. It consists of two rafters with noggins nailed between them.

Wall plate – This transfers the loads imposed on the roof, uniformly over the supporting brickwork. It also provides a bearing and fixing point for the feet of the rafters.

Ceiling joists – As well as being joists on which the ceiling is fixed, they also act as ties for each pair of rafters at wall plate level.

Binders and hangers – These stiffen and support the ceiling joists in their mid-span, to prevent them from sagging and distorting the ceiling.

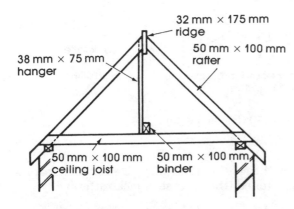

Figure 4.61 Close-couple roof

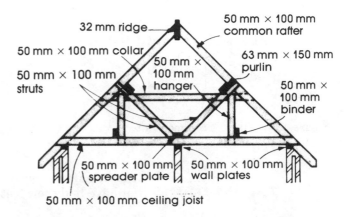

Figure 4.62 Double roof for spans up to 7.2 m

Valley – where two pitched roofs intersect a valley is formed between the two sloping surfaces. This valley may be constructed in one of two ways. Either a valley rafter is used and the feet of the common rafters (cripple rafters) of both roofs are trimmed into it, as shown in Figure 4.63, or the rafters of one roof are run through and lay boards are used to take the feet of the cripple rafters of the other roof as shown in Figure 4.64.

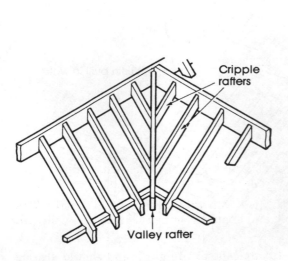

Figure 4.63 Valley using valley rafter

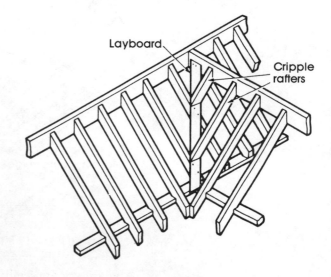

Figure 4.64 Valley using lay board

Trimming – where openings occur in roofs, in either the rafters or ceiling joists or both, these have to be trimmed (see Figures 4.65, 4.66). Framing anchors or housing joints are used to join the trimmers, trimmings and trimmed components together.

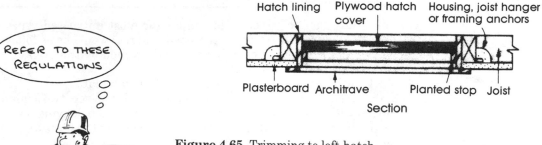

Figure 4.65 Trimming to loft hatch

When trimming around a chimney stack in order to comply with Building Regulations, no combustible material, including timber is to be placed within 200 mm of the inside of the flue lining; or, where the thickness of the chimney surrounding the flue is less than 200 mm, no combustible material must be placed within 40 mm of the chimney.

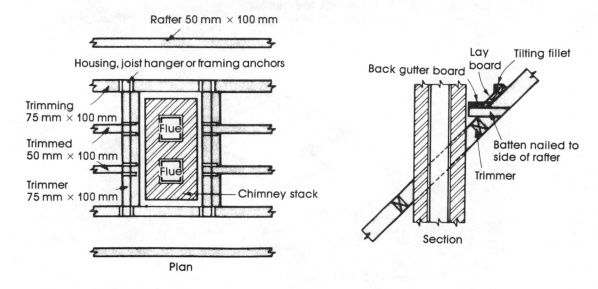

Figure 4.66 Trimming to chimney stack

Anchoring roofs – rafters can be skew nailed to the wall plates or, in areas noted for high winds, framing anchors or truss clips where appropriate can be used.

Wall plates must be secured to the wall with straps at 2 m centres. The rafters adjacent to the gable end should also be tied into the wall with metal restraint straps at 2 m centres.

The rafters and ceiling joists adjacent to the gable end should also be tied into the wall with metal restraint straps at 2 m centres.

Thermal insulation in pitched roofs – can be achieved by placing insulation between the ceiling joists and incorporating a vapour check, such as foil-backed plasterboard, at ceiling level.

Care must be taken not to block the eaves with the insulating material as the roof space must be ventilated.

Roof erection

The procedure for roof erection is similar for most untrussed types of roof. The procedure of erection for a hipped-end roof would be as follows:

1) The wall plate, having been bedded and levelled by the bricklayer, must be tied down.
2) Mark out the position of the rafters on the wall plate.
3) Make up two temporary A-frames. These each consist of two common rafters with a temporary tie joining them at the top, leaving a space for the ridge and a temporary tie nailed to them in the position of the ceiling joists.
4) Fix ceiling joists in position.
5) Stand up the A-frames at either end of the roof in the position of the last common rafter (half span of roof from corner of wall plate to centre line of rafter).
6) Fix temporary braces to hold the A-frames upright.
7) Mark out the spacing of the rafters on the ridge and fix in position (see Figure 4.67).
8) Fix the crown and hip rafters.
9) Fix the purlins, struts and binders.
10) Fix the remaining common rafters and jack rafters.
11) Fix the collars and hangers.
12) Finish the roof at the eaves with fascia and soffit as required.

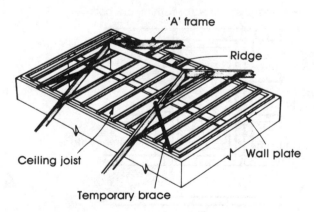

Figure 4.67 Roof erection

Roofing lengths and bevels

Geometry or the use of a roofing square are the two methods mainly used to determine the lengths and bevels required for a traditional cut roof.

Roofing geometry

In this section the geometry required for hipped-end roofs, double roofs and roofs with valleys is covered.

Figure 4.68 is a scale drawing of a part plan and section of a hipped-end roof with purlins. The drawing shows all the developments, angles and true lengths required to set out and construct the roof.

Note: Common abbreviations which may be used have been included in brackets.

The geometry for each of these developments, angles and true lengths are considered separately in the following figures.

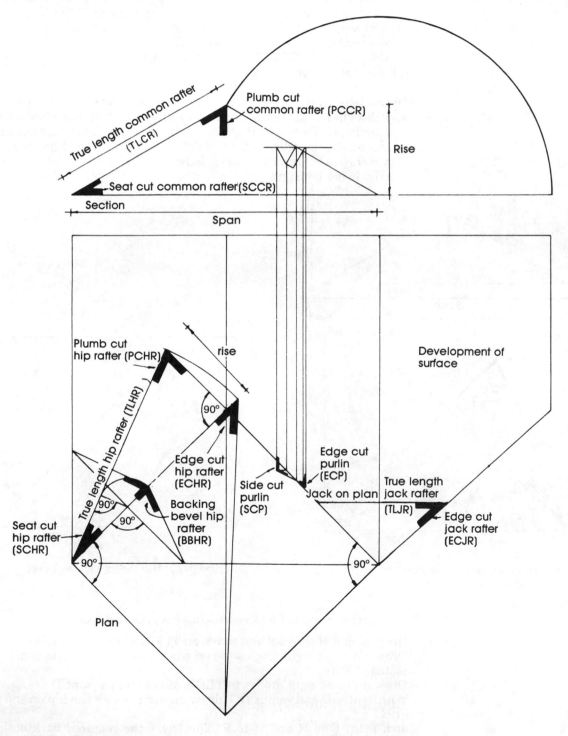

Figure 4.68 Roofing angles and true lengths

Angles and true lengths for the common and hip rafters – shown in Figure 4.69. The method used is as follows:

Draw to a suitable scale, the plan and section of the roof.

Note: On regular plan roofs, the hip rafters will be 45 degrees. On irregular plan roofs the angle will have to be bisected.

Indicate on the section the following:
(a) the true length of the common rafter (TLCR)
(b) the plumb cut for the common rafter (PCCR)
(c) the seat cut for the common rafter (SCCR)
At right angles to one of the hips on the plan, draw line A¹B¹ and mark on it the rise of the roof AB taken from the section.
Join B¹ to C and indicate the following:
(a) the true length for the hip rafter (TLHR)
(b) the plumb cut for the hip rafter (PCHR)
(c) the seat cut for the hip rafter (SCHR)

Diahedral angle or backing bevel for the hip rafter – shown in Figure 4.70. The diahedral angle is the angle of intersection between the two sloping roof surfaces. It provides a level surface for the tile battens or boards on closeboarded roofs to lie flat over the jacks and hips. However, it is rarely used in roofing work today for economic reasons, the edge usually being left square.

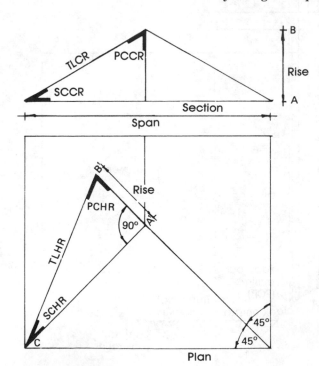

Figure 4.69 Common and hip rafters, angles and true lengths

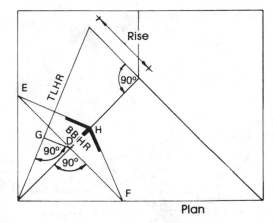

Figure 4.70 Hip rafter backing bevel

The method used to find the backing bevel is as follows:

Draw a plan of the roof and mark on TLHR as before.
Draw a line at right angles to the hip on the plan at D to touch wall plates at E and F.
Draw a line at right angles to TLHR at G to touch point D.
With centre D and radius DG, draw an arc to touch the hip on the plan at H.
Join point E to H and H to F. This gives the required backing bevel (BBHR).

Edge cut to hip rafter – shown in Figure 4.71. This is applied to both sides to allow the hip to fit up to the ridge board between the crown and common rafters.

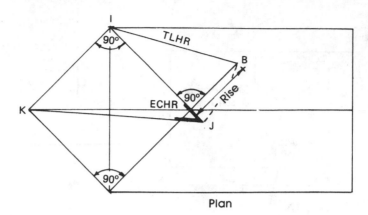

Figure 4.71 Hip rafter edge cut

The method used to find the edge cut is as follows:

Draw a plan of the roof and mark on TLHR as before.
With centre I and radius IB, swing TLHR down to J. (This makes IJ, TLHR.)
Draw lines at right angles from the ends of the hips and extend the ridge line. All three lines will intersect at K.
Join K to J. Angle IJK is the required edge cut (ECHR).

Jack rafter true lengths and edge cut – shown in Figure 4.72. The edge cut allows the jack rafters to sit up against the hip. The plumb and seat cuts for the jacks are those used for the common rafters.

The method used to find the true lengths and edge cut is as follows:

Draw the plan and section of roof. Mark on the plan the jack rafters.
Develop roof surfaces by swinging TLCR down to L and project down to M¹.
With centre N and radius NM¹, draw arc M¹O. Join points M¹ and O to ends of hips as shown.
Continue jack rafters on to development.
Mark the true length of jack rafter (TLJR) and edge cut for jack rafter (ECJR).

Purlin side and edge cut – shown in Figure 4.73. These allow the purlin to sit up against the hip.

The method used is as follows:

Draw a section of the common rafter with purlin and plan of hip.
With centre B and radii BA and BC draw arcs onto a horizontal line to give points D and E.
Project D and E down on to plan.
Draw horizontal lines from A¹ and C¹ to give points D¹ and E¹.
Angle DD¹B¹ is the side cut purlin (SCP) and angle B¹E¹E is the edge cut purlin (ECP).

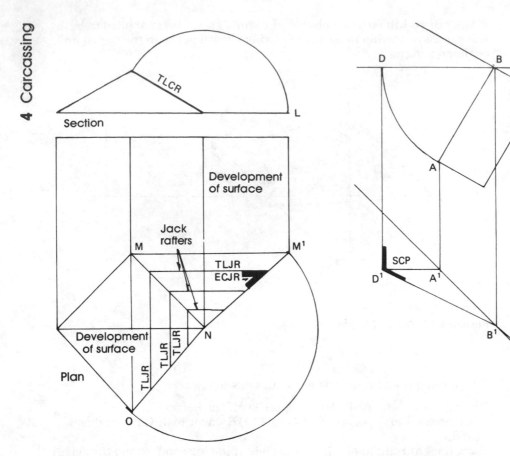

Figure 4.72 Roof development

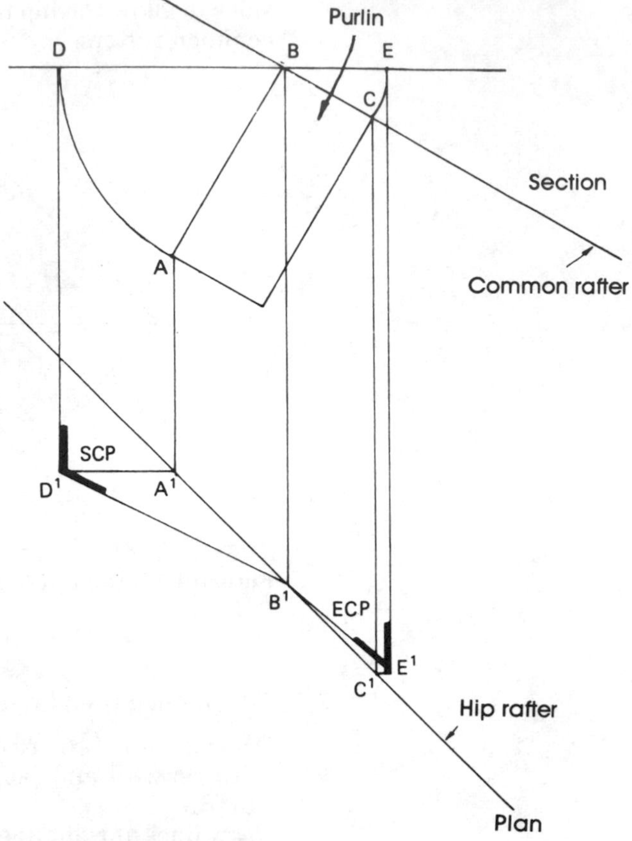

Figure 4.73 Purlin angles

Purlin lip cut – this is required where deep purlins run under the bottom edge of the hip. In practice, this is rarely developed and simply cut in situ on the job.

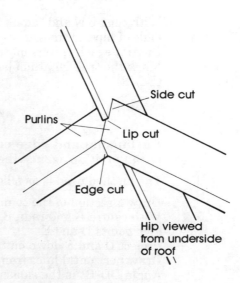

Figure 4.74 Purlin lip cut

Valley lengths and bevels – where two sloping roof surfaces meet at an internal angle, a valley is formed. The true lengths and bevels shown in Figures 4.75–7 can be determined using the same procedure as those used for the hip and jack rafters.

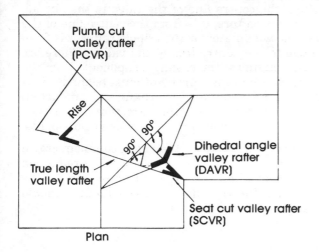

Figure 4.75 Valley rafter, true length and angles

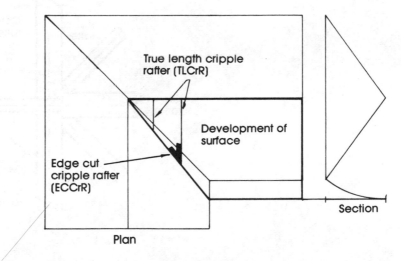

Figure 4.76 Valley rafter edge cut

Figure 4.77 Cripple rafter, true lengths and edge cut

Pitch line – a single line is used in roof geometry to represent the pitch line, this is a line marked up from the underside of the common rafter, one third of its depth.

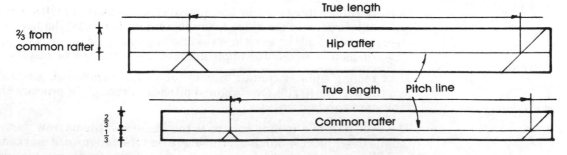

Figure 4.78 Setting out rafters

As the hip and valley rafters are usually of deeper section, the pitch line on these is marked down from the top edge at a distance equal to two thirds the depth of the common rafter.

Allowances – the true length of the common and hip rafters is measured on the pitch line from the centre line of the ridge to the outside edge of the wall plate. For jack rafters, it is from the centre line of the hip to the outside edge of the wall plate; for the cripple rafter it is from the centre line of the ridge to the centre line of the valley. Therefore when marking out the true lengths of the roofing components from the single line drawing, an allowance in measurement must be made. This allowance should be an addition for the eaves overhang and a reduction to allow for the thickness of the components. If this reduction is not apparent, it may be found by drawing the relevant intersecting components.

Figure 4.79 shows the intersection between the ridge, common, crown and hip rafters. The reduction of the hip rafters is shown. The reduction for the common rafters is always half the ridge thickness and for the crown rafter half the common rafter thickness. These reductions should be marked out at right angles to the plumb cut.

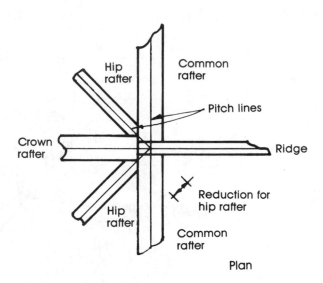

Figure 4.79 Reduction for thickness of materials

Roofing square

Setting out rafters – After having covered geometrically the lengths and angles required for hipped, double and valley roofs, the use of the steel square to find the same lengths and angles should be fairly straightforward, as it is merely the application of the geometric principles.

Most roofing squares contain sets of tables on them which give rafter lengths per metre run for standard pitches, although in practice these tables are rarely used.

The wide part of a roofing square is the blade and the narrow part, the tongue (see Figure 4.80). Both the blade and the tongue are marked out in millimetres. Most carpenters will make a fence for themselves using two battens and four small bolts and wing nuts.

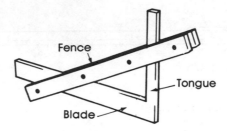

Figure 4.80 Roofing square and fence

To set out a roof using the roofing square, the rise of the roof is set on the tongue and the run of the rafter is set on the blade (run of rafter = half of the span). In order to set the rise and run on the roofing square, these measurements must be scaled down and it is usual to divide them by ten.

Example

For a roof with a rise of 2.5 m and a rafter run of 3.5 m, the scale lengths to set on the roofing square would be:

Rise 2.5 m ÷ 10 = 250 mm
Run 3.5 m ÷ 10 = 350 mm

Figure 4.81 shows how to set up the roofing square and fence to obtain the required lengths and angles. The lengths will, however, be scale lengths.

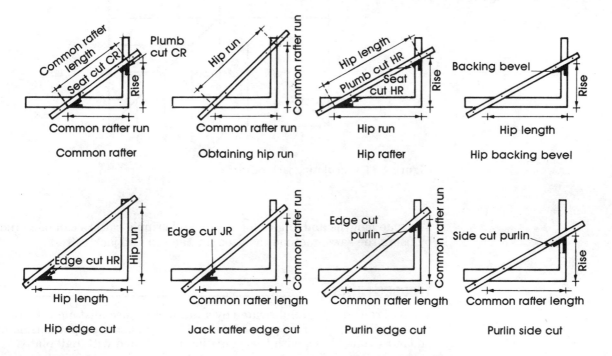

Figure 4.81 Setting up a roofing square to obtain various scale lengths and angles

Figure 4.82 shows how the roofing square may be stepped down the rafter ten times to obtain its actual length. Alternatively, the scale length can be measured off the roofing square and multiplied by ten to give its actual length.

Pitch line 10 9 8 7 6 5 4 3 2 1

Bird's mouth

Plumb cut at ridge
(before cutting do not
forget allowances)

Figure 4.82 Using a roofing square

Allowances – the roofing square like the geometrical method gives the true lengths of members on the pitch line. Therefore the same allowances in measurement as stated before must be made. The length for the shortest jack rafter can be found by dividing the length of the common rafter by one more than the number of jack rafters on each side of the hip. This measurement is then added to each successive jack rafter to obtain its length. For example, for the roof shown in Figure 4.83 with three jack rafters on each side of the hip and a common rafter length of say 2.1 m:

Length of short jack (1)	=	2.1 m ÷ 4
	=	525 mm
Length of middle jack (2)	=	525 mm + 525 mm
	=	1.05 m
Length of long jack (3)	=	1.05 m + 525 mm
	=	1.575 m

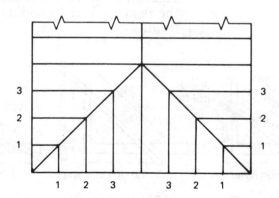

Figure 4.83 Calculating jack rafter lengths

The true lengths and angles for valley and cripple rafters can be found by using the same methods as used for the hip and jack rafters.

Trussed rafters

Trussed rafters are prefabricated by a number of specialist manufacturers in a wide range of shapes and sizes. They consist of prepared timber laid out in one plane, with their butt joints fastened with nail plates.

In use the trusses are spaced along the roof at between 400 mm and 600 mm centres and fixed to the wall plate, preferably using truss clips.

In order to provide lateral stability the roof requires binders at both ceiling and apex level and diagonal rafter bracing fixed to the underside of the rafters (see Figure 4.86). These must be fixed in accordance with the individual manufacturer's instructions.

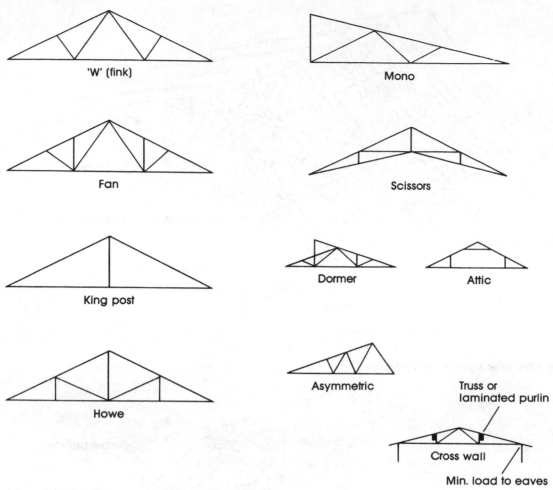

Figure 4.84 Standard trussed rafter configurations

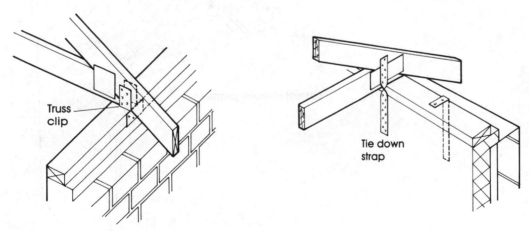

Figure 4.85 Fixing trussed rafters to wall plate

Figure 4.87 shows how the gable wall must be tied back to the roof for support. This is done using lateral restraint straps at 2 m maximum centres both up the rafter slope and along the ceiling tie.

Prefabricated gable ladders (Figure 4.89) are fixed to the last truss when an overhanging verge is required.

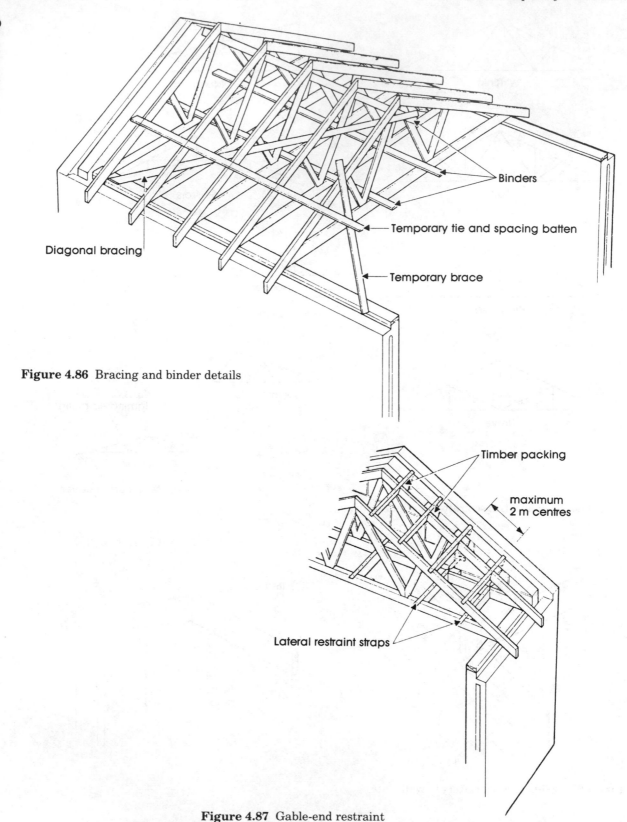

Figure 4.86 Bracing and binder details

Figure 4.87 Gable-end restraint

Where hip ends and valleys occur in trussed rafter roofs, these may be formed either by using loose timber and cutting normal hip and valley rafters, etc., in the traditional manner (see Figure 4.90), or by using specially manufactured components.

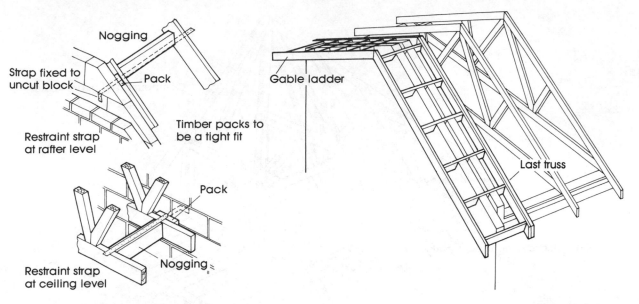

Figure 4.88 is labelled: Nogging; Strap fixed to uncut block; Pack; Timber packs to be a tight fit; Restraint strap at rafter level; Pack; Nogging; Restraint strap at ceiling level

Figure 4.88 Gable tied back to roof for support

Figure 4.89 is labelled: Gable ladder; Last truss

Figure 4.89 Prefabricated gable ladder

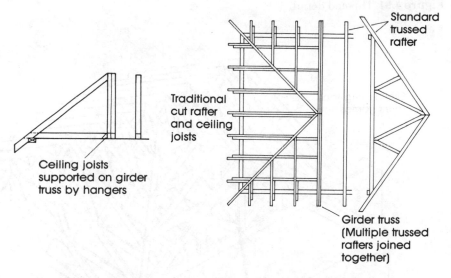

Figure 4.90 is labelled: Standard trussed rafter; Traditional cut rafter and ceiling joists; Ceiling joists supported on girder truss by hangers; Girder truss (Multiple trussed rafters joined together)

Figure 4.90 Traditional cut rafter hip end to trussed rafter roof

Figure 4.91 shows how a hip end may be formed using a compound hip girder truss to support hip mono trusses. Loose hip rafters, infill jack rafters and ceiling joists must still be cut and fixed in the normal way.

Figure 4.92 shows how a valley may be formed where two roofs intersect at a tee junction, using diminishing jack rafter frames nailed on to lay boards. The ends of the rafters on the main roof are carried across the opening by suspending them from the compound girder truss using suitable joist hangers.

Trimming – Wherever possible, openings in roofs for chimney stacks and loft hatches should be accommodated within the trussed rafter spacing. If larger openings are required the method shown in Figure 4.93 can be used. This entails positioning a trussed rafter on either side of the opening and infilling the space between with normal

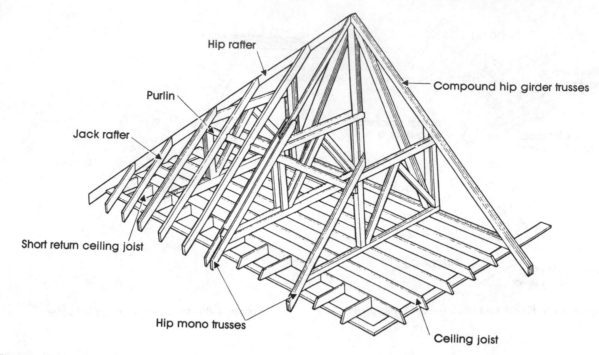

Hip rafter

Purlin

Jack rafter

Compound hip girder trusses

Short return ceiling joist

Hip mono trusses

Ceiling joist

Figure 4.91 Hip-end detail

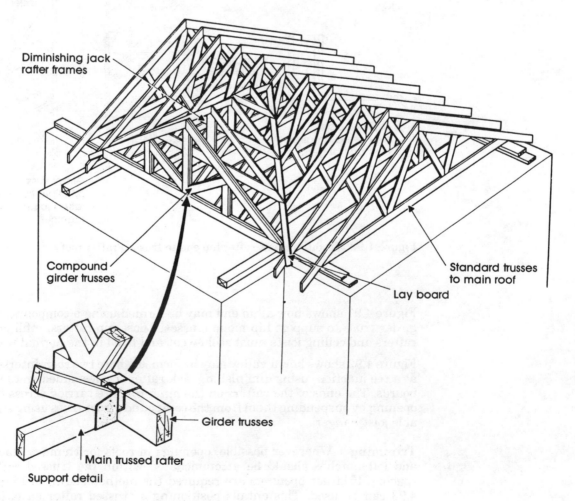

Diminishing jack
rafter frames

Compound
girder trusses

Standard trusses
to main roof

Lay board

Girder trusses

Main trussed rafter

Support detail

Figure 4.92 Valley detail

rafters, purlins and ceiling joists. For safety reasons, on no account should trussed rafters be trimmed or otherwise modified without the structural designer's approval.

Water tank platforms – these should be placed centrally in the roof with the load spread over at least three trussed rafters. The lower bearers of the platform should be positioned so that the load is transferred as near as possible to the mid-third points of the span (see Figure 4.94).

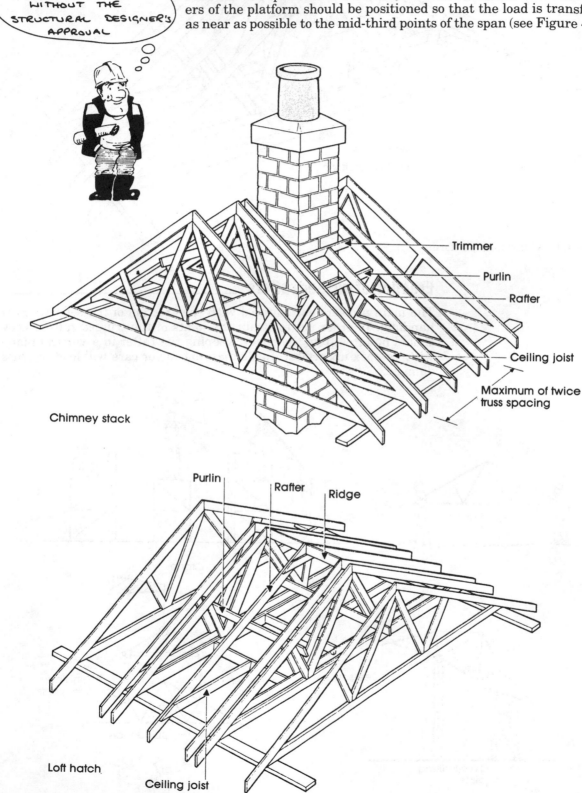

Figure 4.93 Trimming to openings

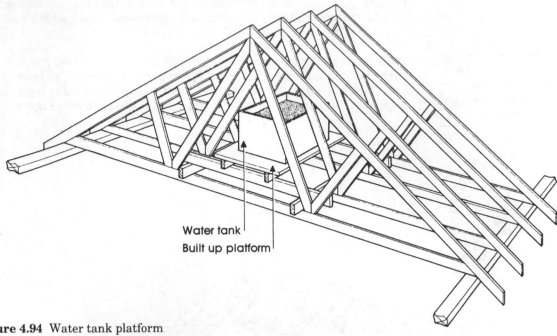

Figure 4.94 Water tank platform

Water tank
Built up platform

Erection of trussed rafters

The main problem encountered with the erection of trussed rafters is handling. In order not to strain the joints of the trussed rafters they should be lifted from the eaves, keeping the rafter in a vertical plane with its apex uppermost. Inadequate labour or care will lead to truss damage.

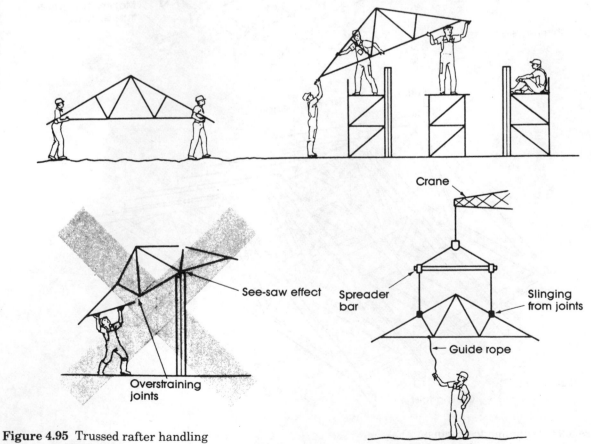

See-saw effect

Overstraining joints

Crane

Spreader bar

Slinging from joints

Guide rope

Figure 4.95 Trussed rafter handling

Trussed rafters may be lifted into position with the aid of a crane, either singly from the node joints using a spreader bar and slings or in banded sets. In both cases these should be controlled from the ground using a guide rope to prevent swinging.

The erection procedure – The erection procedure for a gable end roof using trussed rafters is as follows:
1) Mark the position of the trusses along the wall plates (see Figure 4.96).
2) Once up on the roof, the first trussed rafter can be placed in position at the end of the under-rafter diagonal bracing. It can then be fixed at the eaves, plumbed and temporarily braced.
3) Fix the remaining trussed rafters in position one at a time to the gable end, temporarily tying each rafter to the preceding one with a batten.
4) Fix diagonal bracing and binders.
5) Repeat the previous procedure at the other end of the roof.
6) Position and fix the trusses between the two braced ends one at a time, and fix binders.
7) Fix ladder frames and restraint straps.
8) Finish the roof at the eaves and verge with fascia, bargeboard and soffit as required.

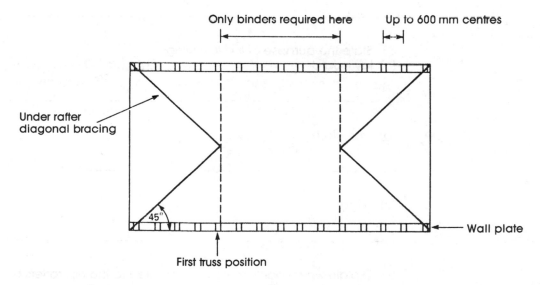

Figure 4.96 Positioning trusses along wall plates

Questions for you

51. Produce a sketch to show the difference between a single and double roof.

52. Define a flat roof.

_____

_____

53. State the purpose of the following:
(a) lay board

_____

(b) wall plate

_____

(c) ridge

_____

54. Explain why a backing bevel is applied to the hip rafters of a close boarded traditional roof.

_____

_____

55. The joint used at the intersection of a rafter and wall plates is:
(a) birdsmouth
(b) splayed dovetail
(c) half lapped joint
(d) butt joint

a	b	c	d
⊏ ⊐	⊏ ⊐	⊏ ⊐	⊏ ⊐

56. Explain the difference between:
(a) hip and valley rafters

_____

_____

(b) jack and cripple rafters

_____

_____

57. Explain the reason why a purlin is incorporated into a roof.

_____

_____

58. Produce a sketch to show and state the purpose of lateral restraint straps used in roofing structures.

WELL, HOW DID YOU DO?

WORK THROUGH THE SECTION AGAIN IF YOU HAD ANY PROBLEMS

WORD-SQUARE SEARCH

Hidden in the word square are the following 20 words associated with '*Timber pitched roofs*'. You may find the words written forwards, backwards, up, down or diagonally.

Trussed	Hipped
Rafter	Flat
Roofs	Horizontal
Valleys	Diagonal
Gables	Framed
Hip	Prefabricated
Binders	Nail plates
Bracing	Lateral
Chevron	Stability
Pitched	Noggins

Draw a ring around the words, or line in using a highlight pen thus:

EXAMPLE

EXAMPLE

C	N	I	D	R	S	Y	E	L	L	A	V	A	C	S	H	D	H
H	E	F	G	H	J	I	L	K	A	O	M	P	F	Q	I	I	S
E	R	G	N	S	N	I	G	G	O	N	U	O	E	W	P	X	Y
V	Z	D	B	D	C	H	E	M	K	X	O	T	O	S	P	S	O
R	A	E	G	A	B	L	E	S	M	R	S	G	P	T	E	E	M
O	C	S	L	O	M	P	R	Y	X	A	M	R	A	B	D	Y	E
N	K	S	B	A	D	I	V	X	B	R	V	K	C	I	E	K	G
T	D	U	P	R	E	F	A	B	R	I	C	A	T	E	D	O	N
I	F	R	N	D	M	F	E	S	P	R	W	T	O	A	M	T	H
O	J	T	K	J	A	I	P	A	E	X	D	Z	E	L	S	O	O
N	J	L	O	P	R	B	E	T	C	E	K	Z	O	T	T	C	R
I	S	T	A	L	F	H	F	G	H	Z	A	P	L	C	A	B	I
N	R	N	Q	R	S	A	K	C	X	Y	Z	B	A	D	B	Q	Z
G	E	O	N	Z	R	G	T	E	K	D	E	O	R	F	I	Z	O
I	D	T	E	P	L	I	X	P	S	D	C	K	E	T	L	X	N
O	N	A	I	L	P	L	A	T	E	S	V	L	T	P	I	S	T
H	I	B	K	S	D	P	R	O	C	K	F	G	A	B	T	Z	A
D	B	R	A	C	I	N	G	V	G	Y	A	S	L	L	Y	U	L

Verge and eaves finishings

Verge, pitched roof

To finish the verge of a gable end roof the ridge and wall plate are extended past the gable end wall, and an additional rafter is pitched to give the required gable overhang. Noggins are fixed between the last two rafters to form a gable ladder. This provides a fixing for the barge board, soffit and tile battens.

Barge board – the continuation of a fascia board around the verge or sloping edge of the roof (typically from 25 mm × 150 mm planed-all-round PAR softwood). It provides a finish to the verge. The lower end of the barge board is usually built up to box in the wall plate and eaves. A template may be cut for the barge board eaves shaping in order to speed up the marking out where a number of roofs are to be cut and also to ensure that each is the same shape (especially where more elaborate designs are concerned).

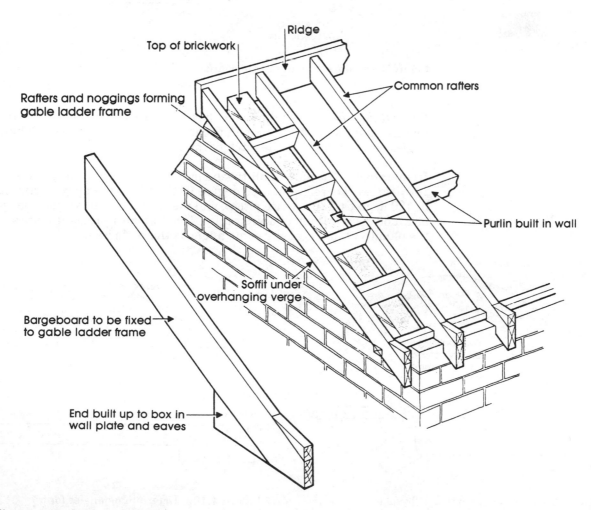

Figure 4.97 Gable-end detail

Two methods may be used for determining the bevels at the apex (top) and foot (bottom) of the barge board:

Marking in position – The board is temporary fixed in position, so a spirit level can then be used to mark the plumb cut (vertical) and seat cut (horizontal) in the required positions (see Figure 4.98).

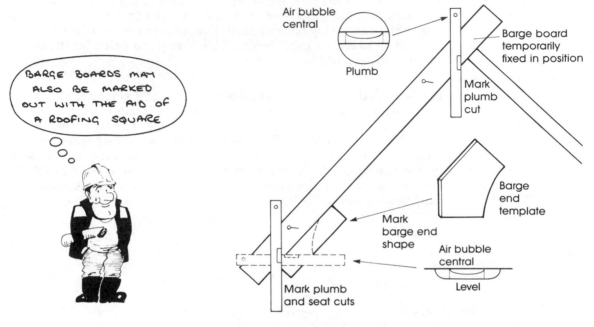

Figure 4.98 Marking out a barge board

Determining bevels – Adjustable bevel squares may be set to the required angles for the plumb and seat cuts, using a protractor. These angles will be related to the pitch of the roof.

Remember – The sum of all three angles in a triangle will always be 180 degrees. Therefore in a 30 degree pitched roof, the apex angle will be 120 degrees (180 – twice pitch), making the plumb cut for each barge board 60 degrees (half of apex angle). The seat cut is at right angles to the plumb cut and is at the same angle as the roof pitch.

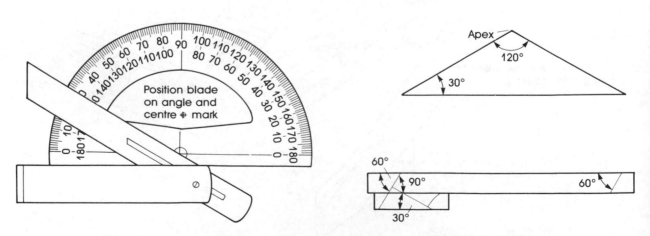

Figure 4.99 Setting an adjustable bevel to a known angle

Figure 4.100 Determining angles for a barge board

READ THE INSTRUCTIONS AND COMPLETE THE TASK

Learning task

Determine and sketch the adjustable bevel set up for the plumb and seat cut angles of a 40 degree pitched roof.

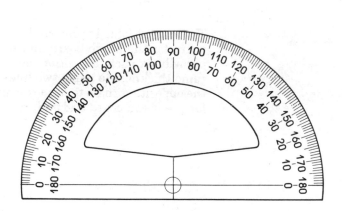

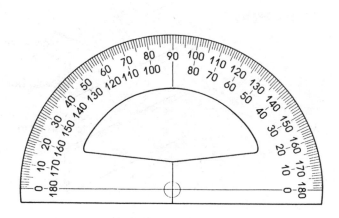

Fixing the barge board – The foot of a barge board may be either mitred to the fascia board, butted and finished flush with the fascia board or butted and extended slightly in front of the fascia board (see Figure 4.101). The actual method used will depend on the specification and/or supervisor's instructions.

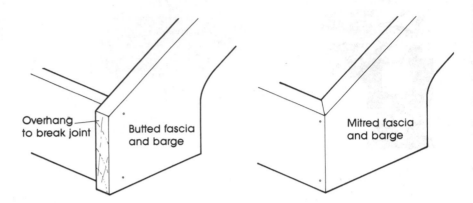

Figure 4.101 Jointing barge to fascia board

The mitred joint is preferred for high quality work. The angle of the mitre for the barge board and fascia is best marked in position. Temporarily fix each in position, one at a time. Use a piece of timber of the same thickness to mark two lines across the edge of the board and join the opposite corners to form the mitre. The face angle will be 90 degrees for the fascia board and a plumb cut for the barge board.

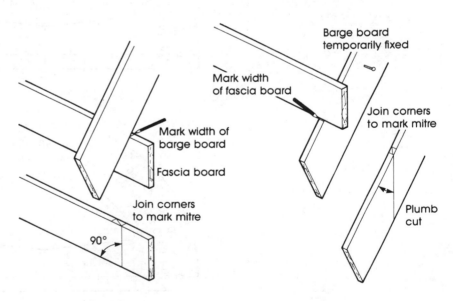

Figure 4.102 Marking barge to fascia board mitre

Where timber of sufficient length is not available for a continuous barge, splayed heading joints may be used as shown in Figure 4.103.

After marking, cutting to shape, mitring and fitting the barge board can be fixed to its gable ladder by double nailing at approximately 400 mm centres. Use either oval nails, wire nails, lost-head nails or cut nails.

These should be at least two and a half times the thickness of the barge board in length in order to provide a sufficiently strong fixing. For example, an 18 mm thick barge board would require nails of at least 45 mm long (50 mm being the nearest standard length). All nails should be punched below the surface ready for subsequent filling by the painter.

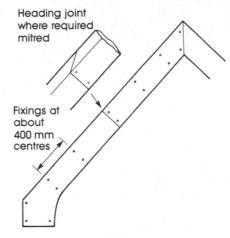

Figure 4.103 Barge board lengthening/fixings

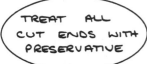

Preservative treatment – It is recommended that all timber used for verge and eaves finishes is preservative treated before use. Any preservative-treated timber cut to size on site will require re-treatment on the freshly cut edges/ends. This can be carried out by applying two brush flood coats of preservative.

Eaves, pitched roof

These may be finished as either:
- flush
- overhanging, open or closed
- sprocketed

Flush eaves – In this method the ends of the rafters are cut off 10–15 mm past the face of the brickwork and the fascia board is nailed directly to them to provide a fixing point for the gutter. The small gap between the back of the fascia board and the brickwork allows for roof space ventilation.

Open eaves – These project well past the face of the wall to provide additional weather protection. The ends of the rafters should be prepared as they are exposed to view from the ground. In cheaper quality work the fascia boards are often omitted and the gutter brackets fixed directly to the side of the rafter.

Closed eaves – These overhang the face of the wall the same as open eaves except that the ends of the rafters are closed with a soffit. Cradling brackets are nailed to the sides of the rafters to support the soffit at the wall edge.

Sprocket piece – Flush, open and closed eaves often use sprocket pieces nailed to the top of each rafter to reduce the pitch of the roof at the eaves. This has the effect of easing the fast flowing rainwater under storm conditions into the gutter.

4 Carcassing

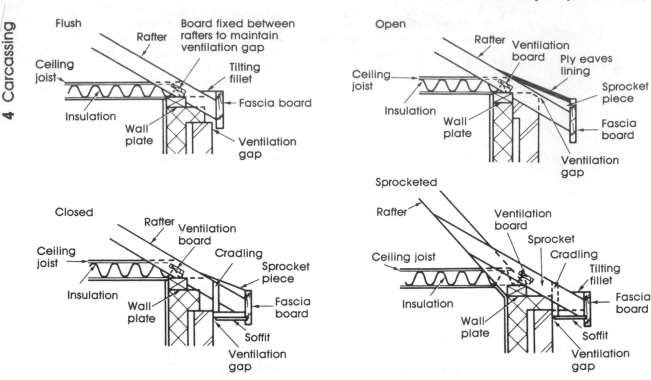

Figure 4.104 Eaves details

Sprocketed eaves – On steeply pitched roofs the flow of rainwater off the roof surface has a tendency to overshoot the gutter. Sprockets can be nailed to the side of each rafter to lower the pitch and slow down the rainwater before it reaches the eaves. This reduces the likelihood of rainwater overshooting the eaves and/or hitting the front of the gutter and splashing back soaking the eaves timbers, with the subsequent risk of rot. In addition the use of sprockets also enhances the appearance of a roof giving it a distinctive 'bell-cast' appearance.

Fascia board – the horizontal board (typically ex 25 mm × 150 mm PAR softwood) which is fixed to the ends of the rafters, to provide a finish to the eaves and a fixing for the guttering.

Before fixing the fascia board the rafter feet will require marking and cutting to plumb and line as shown in Figure 4.105; a seat cut may also be required depending on the assembly detail.
- Measure out from brickwork the required soffit width and mark on the last rafter at either end of the roof.
- Mark the plumb cut and the seat cut if required using a spirit level.
- Stretch a string line between the end two rafters and over the tops of the other rafters, use a spirit level to mark each individual plumb cut.
- Cut the plumb cuts using either a hand or portable circular saw.
- Where a seat cut is required, move the line down to the seat cut position on the end rafters, use a spirit level to mark each individual seat cut.
- Cut the seat cuts using either a hand or portable circular saw.

Where timber of sufficient length is not available for a continuous fascia board, splayed heading joints may be used. Figure 4.106 shows how these should be positioned centrally over a rafter end.

Where level fascia boards are returned around corners it is standard practice to use a mitre at the external and butt at the internal. Both of these joints should be secured by nailing (50 mm ovals).

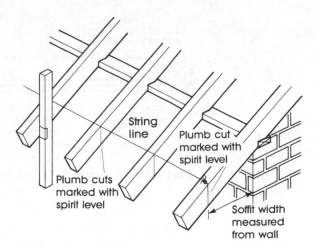

Figure 4.105 Marking out plumb cut at eaves

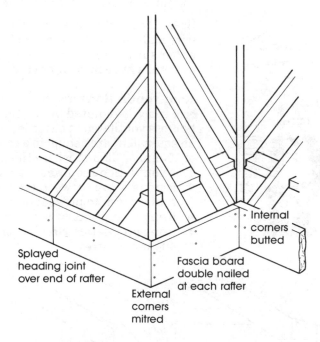

Figure 4.106 Jointing of fascia board

Fascia boards are fixed to the end of each rafter using two nails. These are normally either oval nails, wire nails, lost-head nails or cut nails, at least two and a half times the thickness of the fascia board in length. Typically 50 mm or 62 mm nails provide a sufficiently secure fixing. All nails should be punched below the surface ready for subsequent filling by the painter.

Prior to final fixing the fascia should be checked for line as shown in Figure 4.107.
- Drive nails on the face of the fascia at each end of the roof. Strain a line between them.
- Cut three identical pieces of packing, place one at each end under the line and use the third to check the distance between the fascia and the line at each rafter position.
- Pack out or use a saw to ease ends of rafters as appropriate, so that the packing piece just fits between the fascia and the line.

127

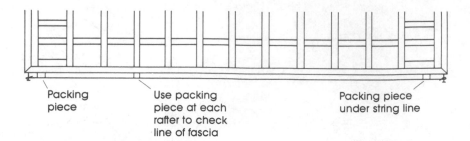

Packing
piece

Use packing
piece at each
rafter to check
line of fascia

Packing piece
under string line

Figure 4.107 Checking fascia board for line

REFER TO THESE
REGULATIONS

Soffit board – used to close the gap between the fascia and the wall of the building, normally either strips of a non-combustible sheet material, hardboard or formed from tongued and grooved matching (T & G). Soffits normally tongue into the fascia board and are fixed to the underside of cleats or L-shaped brackets (cradling) which are themselves fixed to the sides of each rafter at the seat cut line or required soffit line.

Sheet material soffits are typically fixed using two 25 mm galvanised wire nails at each cleat or cradle position. Matchboarded soffits may be either surface nailed or secret nailed through the tongue using 38 mm oval nails at each cleat or cradle position.

Roof ventilation – to reduce the likelihood of condensation within the roof space is required by the Building Regulations 1985. All roofs must be cross ventilated at eaves level by permanent vents. These must have an equivalent area equal to a continuous gap along both sides of the roof of 10 mm or 25 mm where the pitch of the roof is less than 15 degrees. This ventilation requirement can be achieved
- leaving a gap between the wall and soffit (this may be covered with a wire mesh to prevent access by birds, rodents and insects, etc.)
- using a proprietary ventilation strip fixed to the back of the fascia
- using proprietary circular soffit ventilators let into the soffit at about 400 mm centres.

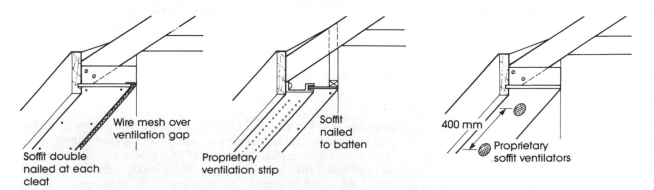

Wire mesh over
ventilation gap

Soffit double
nailed at each
cleat

Proprietary
ventilation strip

Soffit
nailed
to batten

400 mm

Proprietary
soffit ventilators

Figure 4.108 Eaves ventilation

Verge and eaves, flat roofs

The finishing of verge and eaves to flat roofs is a similar process to that of pitched roofs. Both can be finished as either flush or overhanging details as shown in Figures 4.109 and 4.110.

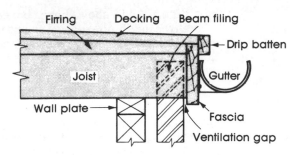

Figure 4.109 Flush eaves

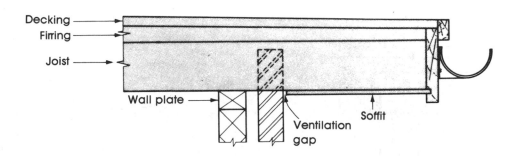

Figure 4.110 Overhanging eaves

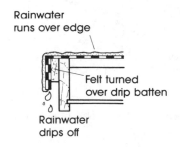

Figure 4.111 Use of drip batten to eaves of flat roof

A drip batten is fixed at the lower eaves, to the top of the fascia to extend the roof edge into the gutter (see Figure 4.111). This extension enables the roofing felt to be turned around it. Rainwater flows off the drip batten into the centre of the gutter, thus ensuring efficient discharge and reducing the risk of rot damage to timber. A drip batten is also fixed at higher eaves and verge edges, again to enable roofing felt to be turned around it. Any moisture is then allowed to drip clear of the fascia and not creep back under the felt by capillary attraction, with the subsequent likelihood of rot.

Capillary attraction, or capillarity, is the phenomenon whereby a liquid can travel against the force of gravity, even vertically in fine spaces or between surfaces placed closely together. This is due to the liquid's own surface tension: the smaller the space the greater the attraction. Measures taken to prevent capillarity, such as forming a drip or groove, are known as anti-capillary measures.

Due to the depth of joists deep fascia boards are often required. These may be formed from solid timber, plywood (WBP, weather and boil proof) or matchboarding. An alternative is to reduce the depth of the joists at the ends by either a splay or square cut as shown in Figure 4.112.

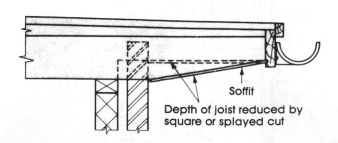

Figure 4.112 Reducing the depth of the joist

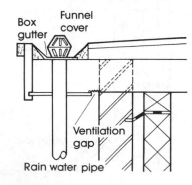

Figure 4.113 Boxed gutter to a flat roof

Figure 4.113 shows how a boxed or internal gutter can be formed at the eaves as an alternative to external gutters. The gutter fall (1 : 60) can be achieved by progressively increasing the depth of cut out in the joists ends towards the outlet.

Angle fillets, as shown in Figures 4.114 and 4.115, are fixed around the upper eaves, verge and edges of the roof which abut brickwork. They enable the roofing felt to be gently turned at the junction; sharp turns on felt lead to cracking, subsequent leaking and risk of rot. In addition the use of angle fillets also prevents rainwater from dripping or being blown over the edges of the roof.

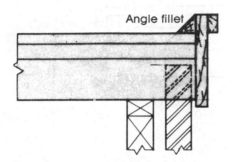

Figure 4.114 Angle fillet at eaves

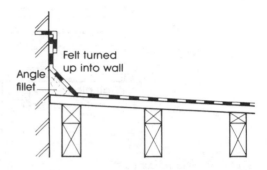

Figure 4.115 Use of an angle fillet to abutments on flat roofs

Overhanging details for the verge and eaves which are positioned at right angles to the main joist run can be formed using two alternative methods:

Returned eaves – short joists are fixed at right angles to the last main joist using joist hangers (see Figure 4.116).

Ladder frame eaves – a ladder frame made from two joists and noggins is made up and fixed to the last joist (see Figure 4.117).

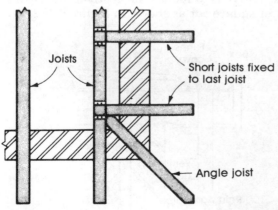

Figure 4.116 Returned eaves

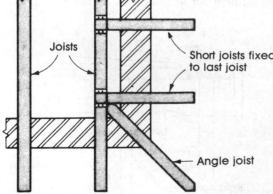

Figure 4.117 Ladder frame eaves

Determining materials

Calculating the lengths of materials required for fascia boards, barge boards and soffits is often a simple matter of measuring, allowing a certain amount extra for jointing, and adding lengths together to determine total metres run.

Example

A hipped-end roof requires two 4.4 m lengths and two 7.2 m lengths of ex 25 mm × 150 mm PAR softwood for its fascia boards.

Metres run required   =   (4.4 × 2) + (7.2 × 2)
                       =   8.8 + 14.4
                       =   23.2 m

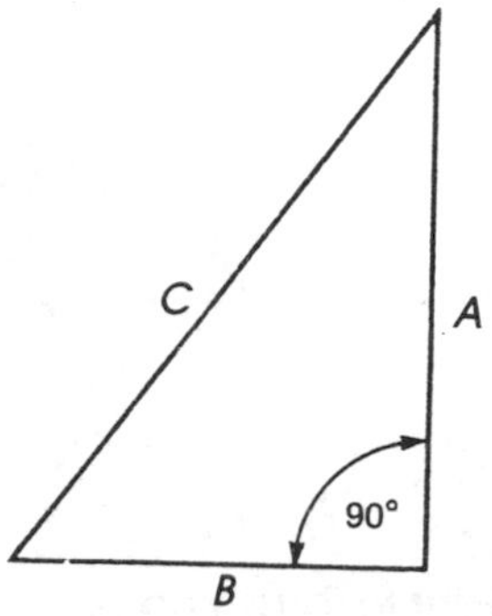

It is standard practice to allow a certain amount extra for cutting and jointing. This is often 10%. 10% of any number can be found by moving its decimal point one place forward. (See also p. 91.)

10% of 23.2 = 2.32

The total metres run of timber is determined by adding the percentage increase to the original number.

Total metres run required   =   23.2 + 2.32
                            =   25.52 m

The length of timber required for barge boards may require calculation using Pythagoras Theorem of right-angled triangles. This states that in any right-angled triangle the square of the hypotenuse (longest side) is equal to the sum of the square of the other two sides. Thus the length of the hypotenuse in a triangle having sides A, B, C is:

$$C = \sqrt{B^2 + A^2}$$

$$A^2 + B^2 = C^2$$

Figure 4.118 Pythagoras's Theorem

Example

Determine the length of barge board required for one gable and having a rise of 3 m and a span of 7 m.

A = Half span = 3.5 m
B = Rise = 3 m
C = Length of barge required for one slope
$C = \sqrt{B^2 + A^2}$
$C = \sqrt{(3 \times 3) + (3.5 \times 3.5)}$
$C = \sqrt{9 + 12.25}$
$C = \sqrt{21.25}$
$C = 4.610$ m

∴ Total length of barge board required for one gable end is 9.220 m.

Where sheet material is used for fascias and soffits the amount which can be cut from a full sheet often needs calculating. This entails dividing the width of the sheet by the width of the fascia or soffit, then using the resulting whole number to multiply by the sheet's length, to give the total metres run.

Example

Determine the total metres run of 150 mm wide soffit board that may be cut from a 1220 mm × 2440 mm sheet.

Number of lengths   =   1220 ÷ 150
                    =   8.133
           say   =   8
Total metres run   =   8 × 2.440
                    =   19.520 m

Learning task

Determine the total amount of ex 50 mm × 225 mm PAR softwood required for the fascia and barge boards and the number of whole 1220 mm × 2440 mm sheets required to cut the 150 mm wide eaves and verge soffit boards. Allow 10% to the total amount as a cutting allowance.

If you are unfamiliar with calculations or simply want to 'brush up' before attempting this learning task, refer to *Carpentry and Joinery for Advanced Craft Students: Site Practice.*

Questions for you

59. Name the regulations which apply to the provision of ventilation in roof spaces.

_____

_____

60. State the purpose of soffit ventilators.

_____

_____

61. Produce sketches to identify the following:
(a) flush eaves

(b) open eaves

(c) closed eaves.

62. State the purpose of a heading joint and produce a sketch of its use in a fascia board.

_____

_____

63. State the purpose of sprockets used in pitched roofs.

_____

_____

64. Produce a sketch to illustrate a sprocket.

65. State the purpose of angle fillets and drip battens used in flat roofs.

_____

_____

_____

_____

66. Produce a sketch to illustrate angle fillets and drip battens.

67. State the reason why the ends of timber sawn on site should be treated with a preservative.

_____

_____

68. Describe the application of preservative on site to a freshly-cut end.

_____

_____

_____

_____

69. Describe each of the following:
(a) fascia board

_____

_____

_____

(b) barge board

_____

_____

(c) soffit board

_____

_____

70. Name a nail suitable for fixing a 6 mm non-combustible sheet material soffit to softwood cradling.

_____

71. Name two nails suitable for fixing an ex 25 mm × 150 mm softwood fascia board to the rafter ends.

_____

_____

72. Name the joint used to return a level fascia board around the external corners of a hipped-end roof.

_____

_____

73. A hipped-end rectangular roof is 14 m long and 7 m wide. Determine:
(a) total length of fascias required

_____

_____

(b) number of 1220 mm × 2440 mm sheets required for the 200 mm wide soffits.

_____

_____

_____

WELL, HOW DID YOU DO?

74. Produce a sketch to illustrate a method of determining the plumb cut required for the upper end of a barge board.

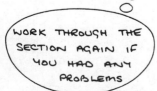

WORK THROUGH THE SECTION AGAIN IF YOU HAD ANY PROBLEMS

WORD-SQUARE SEARCH

Hidden in the word square are the following 20 words associated with *'Verge and eaves finishings'*. You may find the words written forwards, backwards, up, down or diagonally.

Verge	Preservative
Eaves	Plumb cut
Soffit	Seat cut
Gable	Mitre
Hip	Ladder
Roof	Angle fillet
Rafter	Drip batten
Wallplate	Sprocket
Fascia	Ventilation
Barge board	Condensation

Draw a ring around the words, or line in using a highlight pen thus:

EXAMPLE

EXAMPLE

P	R	E	S	E	R	V	A	T	I	V	E	O	R	F	A	C	V
R	E	S	P	L	I	T	H	E	A	D	S	R	A	A	W	O	E
A	R	L	S	L	L	M	F	D	N	D	H	O	F	S	P	P	N
N	I	C	B	A	S	O	F	F	I	T	P	M	T	C	E	O	T
G	A	D	D	A	Y	A	N	E	T	T	C	O	E	I	H	R	I
L	U	V	E	R	G	E	T	G	G	U	C	R	R	A	E	T	L
E	A	N	O	E	P	A	K	U	O	C	D	E	O	I	L	T	A
F	L	W	N	P	E	S	S	L	G	T	S	D	H	O	M	N	T
I	I	T	E	A	V	E	S	A	I	A	O	D	T	A	F	E	I
L	A	C	T	C	C	P	R	T	R	E	S	A	L	E	E	D	O
L	R	O	T	E	K	C	O	R	P	S	H	L	C	I	T	N	N
E	D	N	A	L	E	G	T	O	S	O	A	E	A	O	A	E	W
T	R	S	B	A	R	G	E	B	O	A	R	D	N	N	L	P	A
O	A	T	V	I	U	S	T	S	M	E	R	O	I	C	P	E	E
L	U	R	P	L	U	M	B	C	U	T	I	A	T	I	L	D	R
K	G	A	I	I	E	L	E	T	T	E	R	R	P	D	L	N	T
F	R	C	R	A	S	B	M	L	A	D	E	D	I	R	A	I	I
C	O	N	D	E	N	S	A	T	I	O	N	R	H	G	W	E	M

5 First fixings

In undertaking this chapter you will be required to demonstrate your skill and knowledge of the following first fixing components:
● Timber stud partitions
● Straight flight stairs
● Frames and linings
● Encasing services

You will be required practically to:
● Construct a studwork partition
● Position and fix a straight flight of stairs
● Scribe, position and fix a vertical soil pipe casing
● Position and fix a door lining

Timber studwork partitions

Partition terminology

Partition – an internal wall used to divide space into a number of individual areas or rooms. Partitions are normally of a non-structural/non-load-bearing nature. Figure 5.1 shows how they are commonly formed from either timber studwork framing, proprietary systems or lightweight blockwork.

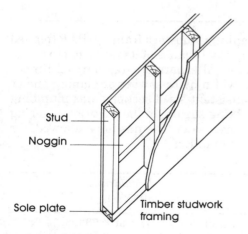
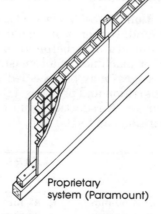
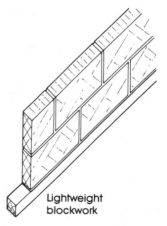

Stud
Noggin
Sole plate
Timber studwork framing
Proprietary system (Paramount)
Lightweight blockwork

Figure 5.1 Partitions

Studwork framing/partition – commonly known as stud partitioning. This is a partition wall built of timber or metal studs, fixed between a sole and head plate, often incorporating noggins for stiffening and fixing (see Figure 5.2).

137

Stud – a vertical timber or metal member of a partition wall fixed between the sole plate and head plate. The main member of a partition, it provides a fixing for the covering material.

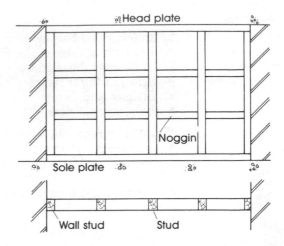

Figure 5.2 Stud partition components

Sole plate/head plate – a horizontal timber fixed above or below studs to provide a fixing point for the studs and ensure an even distribution of loads.

Noggin – a short horizontal piece of timber fixed between vertical studs of a partition. Its use stiffens the studs, provides an intermediate fixing point for the covering material and in addition a fixing point for heavy items which may be hung on the partition (WC cistern, hand basin, etc.).

Timber stud partitions

Traditionally, timber is used for making studwork framing. PAR (planed all round) timber is preferred not only because of its uniform cross section but also it is better to handle. Alternatively, regularised timber (timber machined to a consistent width by re-sawing or planing one or both edges) may be specified. Consistent sized sections aids plumbing of a partition and provides a flat fixing surface of the partition covering materials. A reduction from the basic sawn size has to be allowed, for dimensions up to 100 mm, this is 3 mm. E.g.

Sawn size	PAR size	Regularised size
50 mm × 50 mm	47 mm × 47 mm	47 mm × 50 mm
50 mm × 75 mm	47 mm × 72 mm	50 mm × 72 mm
50 mm × 100 mm	47 mm × 97 mm	50 mm × 97 mm

The standard covering material for partition walls is plasterboard. This is available in 9.5 mm and 12.5 mm thicknesses and in sheet sizes of 900 mm × 1800 mm and 1200 mm × 2400 mm.

Partitions may be constructed in-situ or be pre-made and later erected.

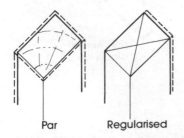

Figure 5.3 Par and regularised sections have a constant width

In-situ partition – Components are cut, assembled and fixed in situation on site.

Pre-made partition – a ready-assembled partition (either on site or in a factory) for later site erection.

Jointing partition members

Traditionally, timber partitions were framed using basic joints, to locate members and provide strength as shown in Figures 5.4 and 5.5. Studs were often housed into the head plate, slotted over a batten at the sole plate and mortised or tenoned at openings. However, present day techniques, calling for speed of erection and economy result in the majority of partitions being simply butt jointed and skew nailed. An alternative to both methods, would be the use of metal framing anchors. These provide a quick yet strong fixing, although they are rarely specified.

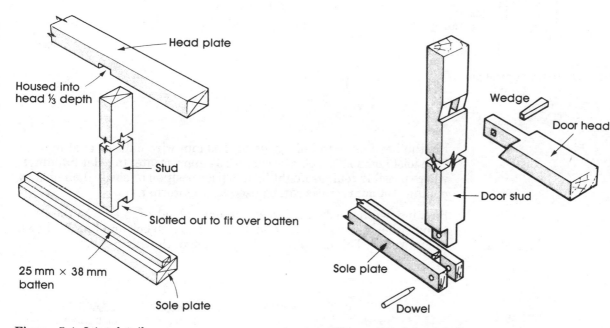

Figure 5.4 Joint details

Figure 5.5 Joint details

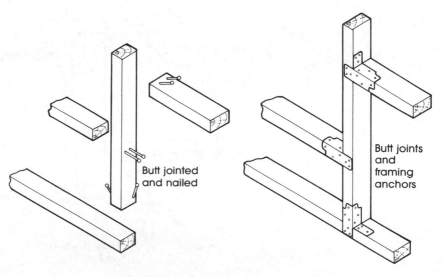

Figure 5.6 Stud partition joints

139

Constructing in-situ stud partitions

Mark the intended position of the partition on the ceiling. Ideally this should either be at right angles to the joists or positioned under a joist or double joist. Where the joists run in the same direction as the partition and it is not directly under a joist, noggins will have to be fixed between joists, to provide a fixing point (see Figure 5.7).

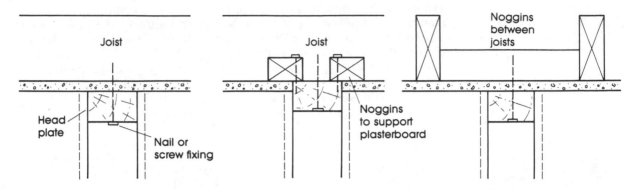

Figure 5.7 Fixing of head plate

Fix the head plate to ceiling, using 100 mm wire nails or oval nails at each joist position or 400 mm centres as appropriate. In older buildings, where possibly ceilings might be in a poor position or easily damaged by nailing, 100 mm screws can be used as an alternative.

Plumb down from the head plate on one side at each end, to the floor, using either a straight edge and level or a plumb bob and line as shown in Figure 5.8. This establishes the position of the sole plate.

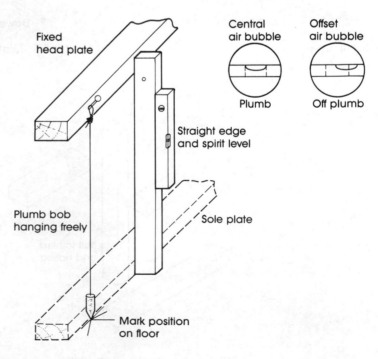

Figure 5.8 Plumbing partition

Fix the sole plate in position with 100 mm wire nails, oval nails or screws as appropriate. Ideally, as with head plates, this should be either at right angles to the joists or over a joist or double joist. Where the joists run in the same direction as the partition but not directly under it, noggins will have to be fixed between joists to provide a fixing point. Where the sole plate is fixed to a concrete floor this should be plugged and screwed.

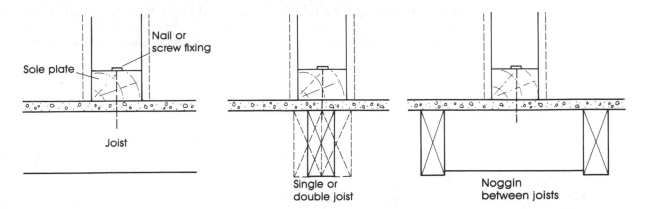

Figure 5.9 Fixing of sole plate

It may be possible to 'shot fix' both head and sole plates to concrete surfaces. However, this is not within the scope of this package. Please refer to *Carpentry and Joinery for Building Craft Students* Book 2 for further information and your supervisor for permission/instruction.

Cut, position and fix the end wall studs. These may be either:
- plugged and screwed to brickwork and blockwork using 100 mm screws into proprietary plugs or twisted timber pallets
- nailed to blockwork or into brickwork mortar joints using 100 mm cut nails
- nailed directly to brickwork using 75 mm hardened steel masonry nails. (It is essential that eye protection is used when driving masonry nails as they are liable to shatter.)

Mark the positions of vertical studs on the sole and head plates. Studs will be required at each joint in the covering material and using 1200 mm wide sheets at 400 mm centres for 9.5 mm plasterboard or at 600 mm centres for 12.5 mm plasterboard; using 900 mm wide sheets, all studs should be at 450 mm centres (see Figure 5.11).

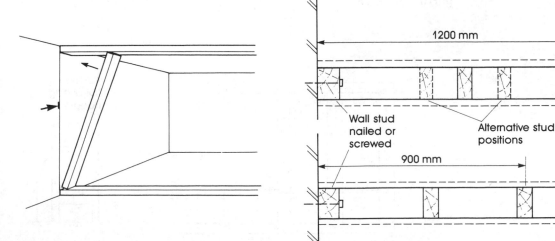

Figure 5.10 Positioning wall stud

Figure 5.11 Stud spacings

Similar centres may be employed for other covering material/cladding. Assuming 12.5 mm × 1200 mm covering, the second stud is fixed with its centre 600 mm from the wall, the third with its centre 1200 mm from the wall and the remaining studs at 600 mm centres thereafter.

Measure, cut and fix each stud to head and sole plates, using 100 mm wire or oval nails, driven at an angle (skew nailed). Each stud should be measured and cut individually as the distance between the plates may vary along their length. Studs should be a tight fit: position one end, angle the stud and drive the other end until plumb. The length of each stud may be measured using either a tape or pinch rods as shown in Figure 5.13.

Figure 5.12 Skew nailing

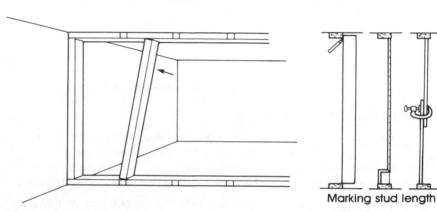

Figure 5.13 Marking and positioning studs

Mark noggin centre line positions; these will vary depending on the specification. Typically they are fixed at vulnerable positions where extra strength is required: at knee height 600 mm up from floor, at waist height 1200 mm up from floor and at shoulder height 1800 mm up from floor. Where deep section skirting is to be fixed a noggin may be specified near its top edge for fixing purposes as shown in Figure 5.14. Additional noggins will also be required where heavy items are to be hung on the wall and where the covering sheet material is jointed in the height of the partition.

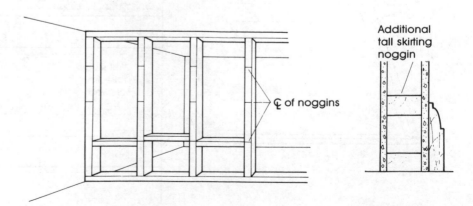

Figure 5.14 Noggin positions

Figure 5.15 shows how to fix the noggins, either by skew nailing using 100 mm wire or oval nails or staggering either side of the centre line and through nailing using 100 mm wire or oval nails.

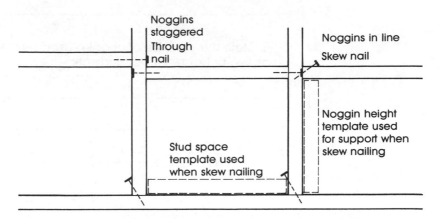

Figure 5.15 Fixing noggins

TRY TO ANSWER THESE

Questions for you

1. State the purpose of a partition wall and name **TWO** methods of construction

_____

_____

_____

_____

2. List **FIVE** component members of timber studwork framing.

_____

_____

_____

_____

_____

3. State the difference between in-situ and pre-made timber stud partitions.

_____

_____

_____

4. State the purpose of noggins used in timber studwork.

_____

_____

5. State the purpose of noggins used between floor joists either above or below timber studwork.

_____

_____

6. Name a nail suitable for fixing a head plate to a timber floor joist.

_____

_____

7. State suitable centres for studs when using 9.5 mm thick × 1200 mm wide plasterboard covering.

_____

_____

8. Name a nail suitable for securing the butt joint between a stud and noggin.

_____

_____

9. Name a nail suitable for securing wall studs directly to brickwork and state any precautions that should be observed in its use.

_____

_____

_____

_____

10. Produce a sketch to illustrate skew nailing.

WELL, HOW DID YOU DO?

WORK THROUGH THE SECTION AGAIN IF YOU HAD ANY PROBLEMS

Estimating materials

To determine the number of studs required for a particular partition the following procedure, shown in Figure 5.16, can be used:

- Measure the distance between the adjacent walls of the room or area which the partition is to divide, say 3400 mm.
- Divide the distance between the walls by the specified stud spacing, say 600 mm. This gives the number of spaces between the studs. Where a whole number is not achieved round up to the whole number above. There will always be one more stud than the number of spaces so add one to this figure to determine the number of studs. Stud centres must be maintained to suit sheet material sizes leaving an undersized space between the last two studs.
- The lengths of head and sole plates are simply the distance between the two walls. Each line of noggins will require a length of timber equal to the distance between the walls.

Example

The total length of timber required for a partition, can be determined by the following method:

7 studs at 2.4 mm, 7 × 2.4	=	16.8 m
Head and sole plates at 3.4 m, 2 × 3.4	=	6.8 m
3 lines of noggins at 3.4 m, 3 × 3.4	=	10.2 m
Total metres run required, 16.8 + 6.8 + 10.2	=	33.8 m

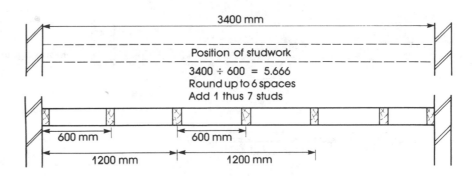

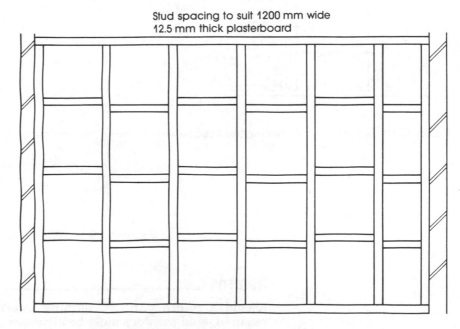

Figure 5.16 Estimating materials for a stud partition

Openings

Where door, serving hatch or borrowed light (internal glazed opening) openings are required in a studwork framing, studs and noggins should be positioned on each side to form the opening. The sole plate will require cutting out between the door studs. Linings are fixed around the framed opening to provide a finish and provision for hanging doors or glazing.

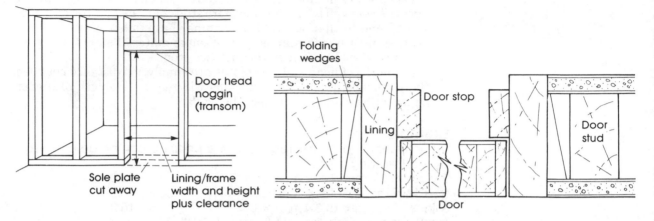

Figure 5.17 Door opening in a stud partition

Figure 5.18 Typical horizontal section of door opening

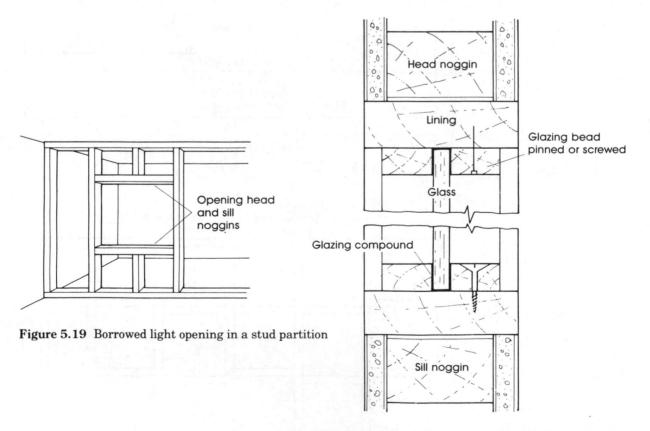

Figure 5.19 Borrowed light opening in a stud partition

Figure 5.20 Typical vertical section of borrowed light

Returns

Should a return partition forming internal or external angles be required, stud positions must be arranged to suit. Consideration must be given to providing a support and fixing for the covering material around the return intersection. Two alternative methods, shown in Figures 5.21 and 5.22, are commonly employed. The particular method adopted will depend on whether the carpenter is fixing the covering material as the work proceeds or the plasterer is fixing it after the carpentry work is complete.

Note: plasterboard has two faces. It should be fixed ivory face outwards for dry lining (not plastered e.g. joints filled and then decorated) or grey face outwards for skimming with plaster (grey face provides good adhesion for plaster skim coat).

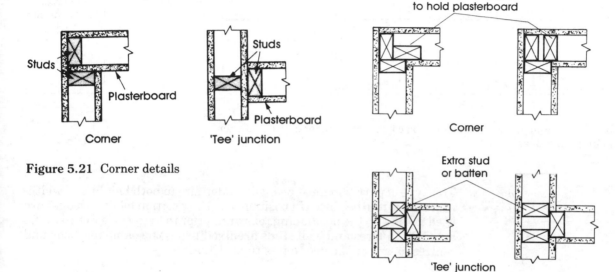

Figure 5.21 Corner details

Figure 5.22 Stud treatment to provide support for coverings at returns

Plasterboard sheets are secured to the studs using plasterboard nails at approximately 150 mm centres around the sheet edges and intermediate studs. To avoid distortion, nailing should commence from the centre of the sheet working outwards. Nails should be driven just below the surface, but taking care not to break or damage the paper face of the sheet.

Wall plates in long partitions and those containing return intersections will require joining preferably using halving joints secured with screws.

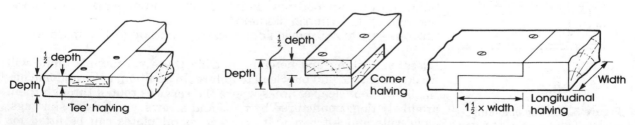

Figure 5.23 Sole and head plate joints

Pre-made partitions

These may be made either by the joiner in a workshop or by the carpenter on site. The method of jointing will normally be either: studs housed into plates with noggins butt-jointed and nailed, or all joints butted and nailed. In addition, occasionally pre-made partitions may be jointed using framing anchors.

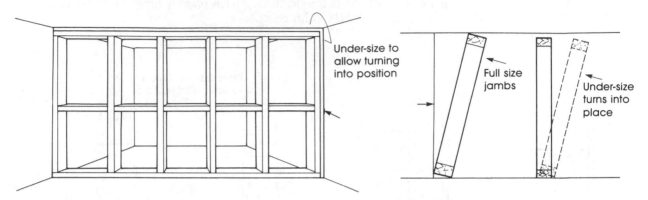

Figure 5.24 Pre-made partitions must be constructed undersize to allow for positioning tolerances

This type of partition must be made under-size in both height and width, in order for it to be placed in position. Once in position folding wedges are used to take up the positioning tolerance prior to fixing (see Figures 5.24 and 5.25). Plates and wall studs are fixed using the same methods and centres as are applicable to in-situ partitions.

Drilling and notching partitions

Service cables and pipes for water, gas and electricity are often concealed within stud partitions. In common with floor joists the positioning of holes and notches in studs has an effect on strength. It is recommended that holes and notches in studs should be kept to a minimum and conform to the following.

Holes – of up to 0.25 of the stud's width, drilled on the centre line (neutral stress line) and located between 0.25 and 0.4 of the stud's height from either end are permissible. Adjacent holes should be separated by at least three times their diameter measured centre to centre.

Notches – on either edge of the stud up to 0.15 of the stud's width and located up to 0.2 of the stud's height from either end are permissible.

Example

The position and sizes for holes and notches in 100 mm width studs, 2400 mm in length are:

Holes – between 600 mm and 960 mm in from either end of the stud and up to 25 mm in diameter.

Notches – up to 480 mm in from each end and up to 15 mm deep.

Excessive drilling and notching outside these permissible limits will weaken the stud and may lead to failure. In addition, holes and notches should be kept clear of areas where the services routed through them are likely to get punctured by nails and screws, e.g. behind skirtings, dado rails and kitchen units etc., or metal plates can be fitted for protection.

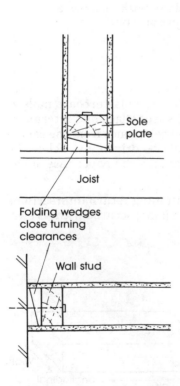

Figure 5.25 Use of folding wedges to take up positioning tolerances

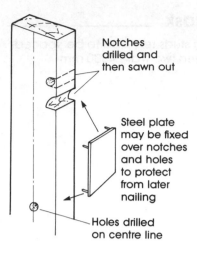

Notches drilled and then sawn out

Steel plate may be fixed over notches and holes to protect from later nailing

Holes drilled on centre line

Figure 5.26 Hole and notch details

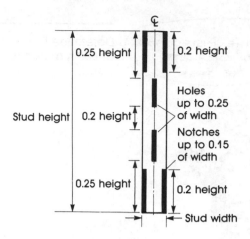

0.25 height — 0.2 height

Stud height — 0.2 height

Holes up to 0.25 of width

Notches up to 0.15 of width

0.25 height — 0.2 height

Stud width

Figure 5.27 Positioning and protection of holes and notches to accommodate services

Fire resistance, thermal insulation and sound insulation

REFER TO THESE REGULATIONS

Depending on the partition's location it may be required to form a fire resisting and/or a thermal insulating and/or a sound insulating function. Specific requirements and methods of achieving them are controlled by the Building Regulations 1985 which should be referred to for information as may be required. However, the general principles for achieving these functions are:

- *Fire resistance* can be increased by a double covering of plasterboard, the second outer layer being fixed so that the joints overlap those in the lower layer.
- *Thermal insulation* can be increased by filling the space between studs with either mineral wool or glassfibre quilt.
- *Sound insulation* can be increased by a discontinuous construction to avoid impact and vibration and the use of lightweight infilling material such as mineral or glassfibre quilt to absorb sound energy.

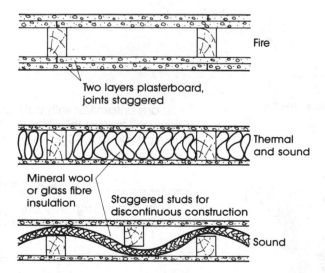

Fire

Two layers plasterboard, joints staggered

Thermal and sound

Mineral wool or glass fibre insulation

Staggered studs for discontinuous construction

Sound

Figure 5.28 Insulation of stud partitions

Learning task

Determine the number of 2400 mm long studs required to be spaced at 600 mm centres, for a partition between two walls 4500 mm apart.

Determine the total amount of timber required in metres run for the partition. Include head plate, sole plate, studs and three lines of noggins.

If you are unfamiliar with calculations or simply want to 'brush up' before attempting this learning task, refer to *Carpentry and Joinery for Advanced Craft Students: Site Practice.*

Questions for you

11. State the reason why pre-made partitions are constructed shorter than the height of the room where they are to be fixed.

_____

_____

12. Produce a sketch to show a suitable means of jointing a sole plate at a return.

13. A stud partition wall is to be dry lined. Which face should be fixed outwards?

_____

_____

14. State the purpose of drilling or notching studs.

_____

_____

15. State the maximum size hole that should be drilled in a 100 mm wide stud.

_____

16. Name the regulations which govern fire resistance, thermal insulation and sound insulation of partitions.

_____

_____

17. Name **TWO** methods of securing glazing beads to the lining of a borrowed light.

_____

_____

18. Determine the total length of timber in metres run required for the following partition:

Eleven 50 mm × 75 mm studs 2400 mm long
Head and sole plate 4100 mm long
Three lines of noggins

_____

_____

_____

_____

WELL, HOW DID YOU DO?

WORK THROUGH THE SECTION AGAIN IF YOU HAD ANY PROBLEMS

151

WORD-SQUARE SEARCH

Hidden in the word square are the following 20 words associated with '*Constructing Studwork Framing*'. You may find the words written forwards, backwards, up, down or diagonally.

Notches	Sound
Wall stud	Insulation
Stud	Intermediate
Partition	Door
Noggin	Lining
Head plate	In situ
Sole plate	Pre-made
Framing	Skew nail
Plasterboard	Wire nail
Thermal	Paramount

Draw a ring around the words, or line in using a highlight pen thus:

(EXAMPLE)

EXAMPLE

```
P L A S T E R B O A R D O F F A C I
R U S P L I T H E A D S E H C T O N
O R T L I N I N G N D H O M N P P T
P I C L A D D E R L C P M B I E O E
I A D F R A M I N G E C O O G H R R
N U W I R E N A I L T C S R G E T M
S K E W N A I L U O A D O A O L T E
U L W A L L S T U D L O A H N M E D
L I O O S U S T A I D N U O S E D I
A A E O T C P R U R E S I L E T A A
T R T R N H O G I D L T O C I S M T
I D A E U E G T O S I A E A O T E E
O R L P O N D A N T H E R M A L R A
N A P V M U S T R M E R O I C C P R
L U D C A U P A E I N S I T U O D D
K G A T R E P E T T E R R O D C N V
F R E T A S B M L A D E D E R S I E
B S H B P A S O L E P L A T E O E L
```

Stairs

A stairway can be defined as a series of steps (combination of tread and riser) giving floor-to-floor access. Each continuous set of steps is called a flight. Landings are introduced between floor levels either to break up a long flight, giving a rest point, or to change the direction of the stair.

Straight-flight stairs

These run in one direction for the entire length. Figure 5.29 shows there are three different variations.

The flight which is closed between two walls (also known as a cottage stair) is the simplest and most economical to make. Its handrail is usually a simple section fixed either directly on to the wall or on brackets.

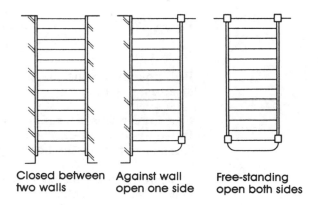

Closed between two walls   Against wall open one side   Free-standing open both sides

Figure 5.29 Straight-flight stairs

The flight fixed against one wall is said to be open on one side. This open or outer string is normally terminated and supported at either end by a newel post. A balustrade must be fixed to this side to provide protection. The infilling of this can be either open or closed and is usually capped by a handrail. Where the width of the flight exceeds one metre, a wall handrail will also be required.

Where the flight is freestanding, neither side being against a wall, it is said to be open both sides. The open sides are treated in the same way as the previous flight.

Stair terminology

Apron lining – the boards used to finish the edge of a trimmed opening in the floor.

Balustrade – the handrail and the infilling between it and the string, landing or floor. This can be called either an open or closed balustrade, depending on the infilling.

Baluster – the short vertical infilling members of an open balustrade.

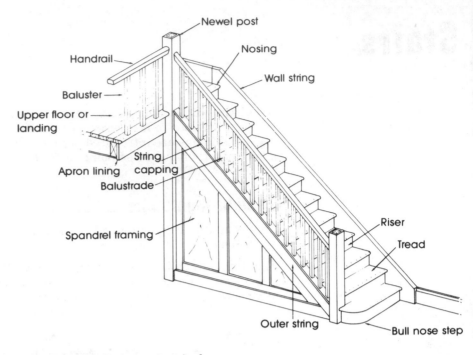

Figure 5.30 Stairway terminology

Bull nose step – the quarter-rounded end step at the bottom of a flight of stairs.

Carriage – This is a raking timber fixed under wide stairs to support the centre of the treads and risers. Brackets are fixed to the side of the carriage to provide further support across the width of the treads.

Commode step – a step with a curved tread and riser normally occurring at the bottom of a flight.

Curtail step – the half-rounded or scroll-end step at the bottom of a flight.

Newel – the large sectioned vertical member at each end of the string. Where an upper newel does not continue down to the floor level below it is known as a pendant or drop newel.

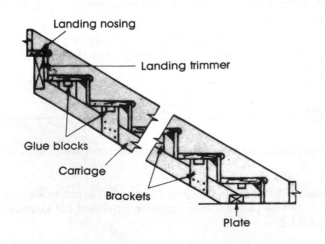

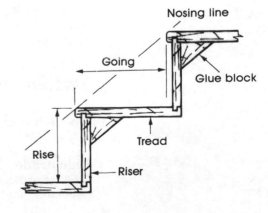

Figure 5.31 Stair carriage

Figure 5.32 Stairway definitions

Nosing – the front edge of a tread or the finish to the floorboards around a stairwell opening.

Riser – the vertical member of a step.

Spandrel – the triangular area formed under the stairs. This can be left open or closed in with spandrel framing to form a cupboard.

String – the board into which the treads and risers are housed or cut. They are also named according to their type, for example, wall string, outer string, close string, cut string, and wreathed string.

Tread – the horizontal member of a step. It can be called a parallel tread or a tapered tread, etc., depending on its shape.

Stair installation

Stairs are normally delivered to site assembled as far as possible, but for ease of handling each flight will be separate. Its newels, handrail and balustrade are supplied loose, ready for on-site completion.

For maximum strength and rigidity the stairs should be fixed as shown in Figures 5.33–6. The top newel is notched over the landing or floor trimmer and either bolted or coach screwed to it. The lower newel should be carried through the landing or floor and bolted to the joists. The lower newel on a solid ground floor can be fixed by inserting a steel dowel partly into the newel and grouting this into the concrete.

The outer string and handrail are mortised into the newels at either end. With the flight in position, these joints are glued and then closed up and fixed using hardwood draw pins. The wall string is cut over the trimmer at the top and cut-nailed or screwed to the wall from the underside. The bottom riser of a flight may be secured by screwing it to a batten fixed to the floor.

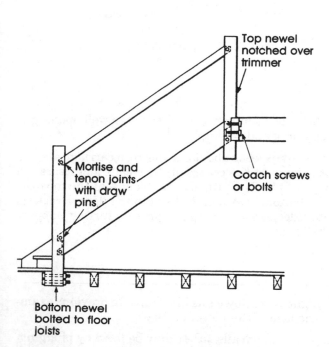

Figure 5.33 Fixing outer string and handrail

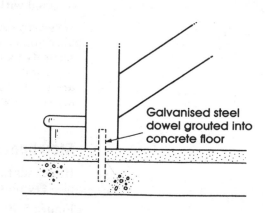

Figure 5.34 Newel fixing

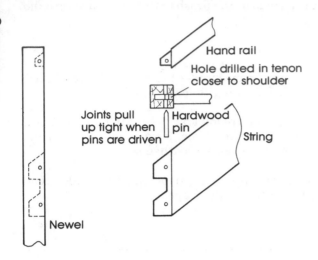

Figure 5.35 String handrail to newel joints

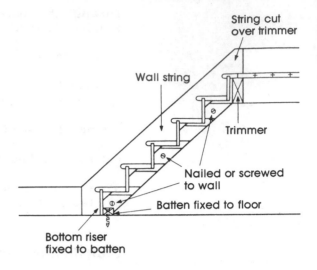

Figure 5.36 Fixing wall string

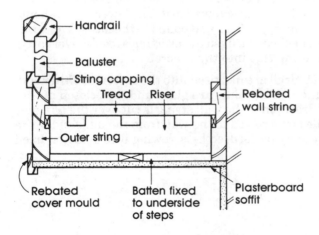

Figure 5.37 Section across flight open one side

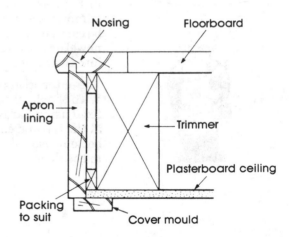

Figure 5.38 Landing detail

Figure 5.38 shows how the trimmer around the stairwell opening is finished with an apron lining and nosing.

Where the width of the stair exceeds about one metre, a carriage may be fixed under the flight to support the centre of the treads and risers. To securely fix the carriage it is birdsmouthed at both ends, at the top over the trimmer and at the bottom over a plate fixed to the floor. Brackets are nailed to alternate sides of the carriage to provide further support across the width of the treads.

Stair handrails

Handrails to straight flights with newels as illustrated in previous examples are tenoned into the face of the newel posts.

Figure 5.39 shows how wall handrails either may be fixed by plugging, screwing and pelleting direct to the wall, or may stand clear of the wall on metal brackets fixed at about one metre centres.

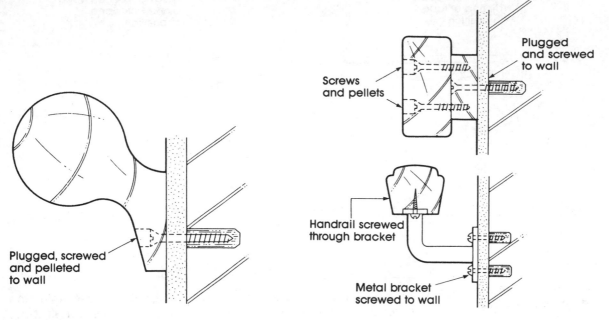

Figure 5.39 Handrail sections

A half newel can be used to give support to the handrail and balustrade where it meets the wall or a landing (see Figure 5.40).

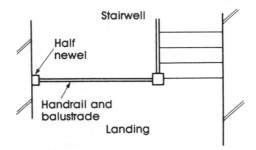

Figure 5.40 Use of half newel

Protection of completed work

After a new staircase has been installed, a short period spent taking measures to prevent damage during subsequent building work saves much more than it costs.

False treads made from strips of hardboard or plywood, as shown in Figure 5.41, are pinned on to the top of each step. The batten fixed to the strip ensures the nosing is well protected. On flights to be clear finished the false treads should be held in position with a strong adhesive tape, as pin holes would not be acceptable.

Strips of hardboard or plywood are also used to protect newel posts. These can be either pinned or taped in position depending on the finish (see Figure 5.42). Adequate protection of handrails and balustrades can be achieved by wrapping them in corrugated cardboard held in position with adhesive tape.

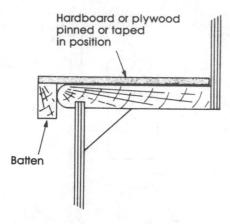

Hardboard or plywood
pinned or taped
in position

Batten

Figure 5.41 Temporary protection of treads

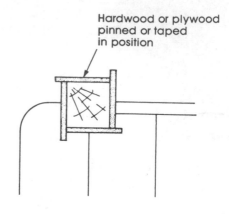

Hardwood or plywood
pinned or taped
in position

Figure 5.42 Temporary protection of newels

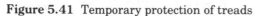

READ THE INSTRUCTIONS
AND COMPLETE
THE TASK

_____ **Learning task** _____

Using the extract from a stair manufacturer's brochure, determine the number of balusters (spindles) required to construct the balustrade shown in the example.

S T A I R P A R T S

HELPFUL HINTS

When calculating the number of 32mm spindles needed on the staircase itself, allow 2 spindles per tread and 1 per tread where there is a newel.

On the landing, to calculate the number of spindles required, (X) simply use the following formula:

$$X = \frac{\text{Horizontal distance (in mm) on landing between newels}}{112}$$

Example

■ Newel Post

NEWELS AND HALF NEWELS

NT 22(M)
NT 21 HALF(M)
NB 635 HALF(M)
NB 635(M)
NT 21(M)
NT 20(M)
NT 19(M)
NB 915(M)

SPINDLES

REGENCY RM 090(M)
GEORGIAN GM 090(M)

NEWEL CAPS

NC 1(M)
NC 2(M)
NC 3(M)

HALF CAPS
NC 1 HALF(M)
NC 2 HALF(M)
NC 3 HALF(M)

HANDRAILS, BASERAILS AND HORIZONTAL TURN

HM 08(M)
HM 12(M)
HM 14(M)

BM 08(M)
BM 12(M)
BM 14(M)

HM (M)

BRACKETS

BB
TB
LB
HB

FILLETS & PLUG

FS(M)
DP(M)

RAILS

NEWEL CAPS

SPINDLES
STRING
NEWEL CENTRES
NEWEL BASES

900 mm min
90 mm max

CUTTING GUIDE & HOLESAW

CG
HS

LANDING

80mm max

BRASS WALL BRACKET

BWB

900mm min

ALL TIMBER STAIRPARTS ARE AVAILABLE IN HEMLOCK AND MAHOGANY (M)

Reproduced with the permission of Richard Burbidge Ltd, Whittington Road, Oswestry, Shropshire SY11 1HZ.
For further information please telephone 0691 655131.

Questions for you

19. List **FIVE** components which may be used in a flight of stairs.

_____

_____

20. Produce a sketch to show how a newel post may be fixed to the landing trimmer.

21. Name the vertical member used to provide support to a handrail and infill an open balustrade.

_____

22. List **THREE** measures that can be taken after stair installation to prevent damage to a flight during building work.

_____

_____

_____

Frames and linings

Terminology

Frame – an assembly of components to form an item of joinery, such as a door or window; a structural framework of columns and beams or panels in steel reinforced concrete or timber.

Lining – the thin covering to door or window reveals; sheet material used to cover wall surfaces.

Door frame – the surround on which an external door or internal door is hung consisting of two jambs, a head and sometimes a threshold and transom; normally with stuck-on solid stops and of a bigger section than door linings.

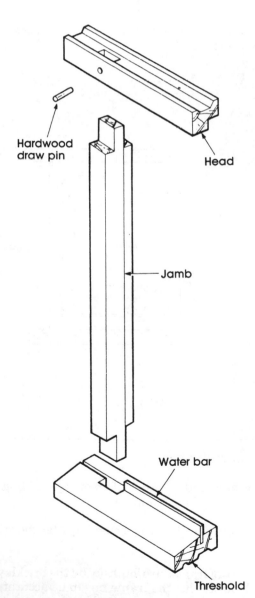

Figure 5.43 Door frame

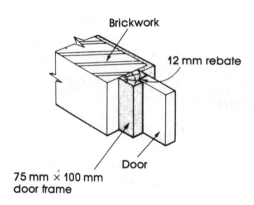

Figure 5.44 Door frame

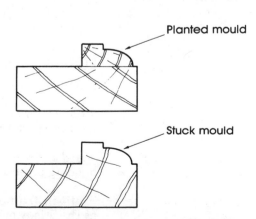

Figure 5.45 Stuck-on and planted stops

Door lining – the surround on which mainly internal doors are hung, normally of a thinner section than door frames and often have planted stops. The main difference between door frames and door linings is that linings cover the full width of the reveal in which they are fixed, from wall surface to wall surface whereas frames do not.

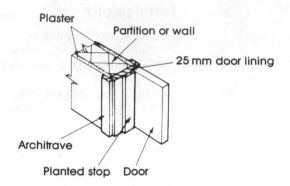

Figure 5.46 Door lining

Window frame – the part of a window that is fixed into the wall opening and receives the casements or sashes.

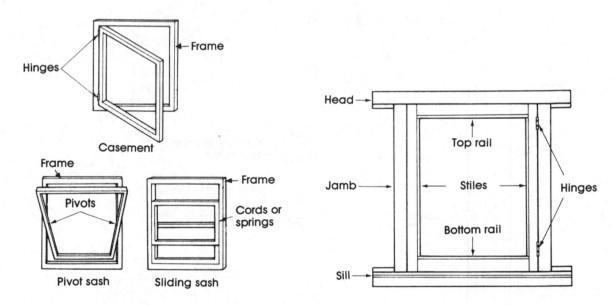

Figure 5.47 Window terminology

Frames

Frames can be either 'built in' or 'fixed in'.

'Built-in' frames are fixed into a wall or other element by bedding in mortar and surrounded with the walling components.

'Fixed-in' frames are inserted into a ready formed opening after the main building process.

'Built-in' frames – the majority of frames are 'built-in' by the bricklayer as the brickwork proceeds. Prior to this the frame has to be accurately positioned, plumbed, levelled and temporary strutted by the carpenter.

Door frames are normally built into the brickwork as the work proceeds. Temporary struts are used to hold the frame upright. The foot of the door frame jambs, in the absence of a threshold, are held in position by galvanised metal dowels which are drilled into the end of the jambs and are grouted into the concrete. This is shown in Figure 5.48. Temporary braces and distance pieces are fixed to the frame, in order to keep it square and the jambs parallel during the 'building-in' process. The vertical positioning of external door and window frames can be achieved with the use of a storey rod shown in Figure 4.26, p. 77.

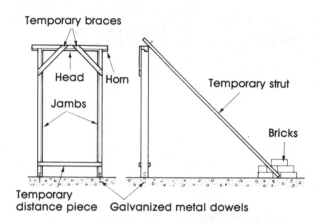

Figure 5.48 'Building in' a frame

A frame's head should be checked for level, and packed up as required; frames with thresholds are normally bedded level using bricklayer's mortar (see Figure 5.49).

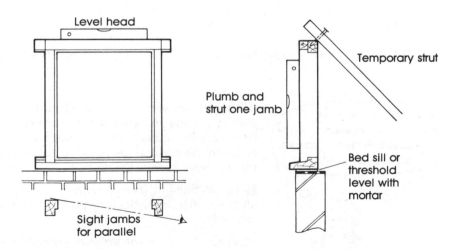

Figure 5.49 Positioning 'built-in' frames

Jambs should be plumbed from the face. It is standard practice to plumb and fix the first using a spirit level. The other is then sighted parallel: stand to the side of the frame, close one eye, sight the edge of the plumbed jamb with the edge of the other and adjust if required until both jambs are parallel.

As the brickwork proceeds galvanised metal frame cramps, as shown in Figure 5.50, should be screwed to the back of the jambs and built into the brickwork. Three or four cramps should be evenly spaced up each jamb.

Figure 5.50 Attaching frame cramps

163

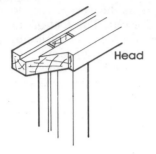

Figure 5.51 Horn cut back ready for 'building in'

The horns of the frame should be cut back as shown before 'building in', rather than cut off flush (see Figure 5.51). The horns will then help to fix the frame in position. After trimming the horns it is essential that the cut ends are treated with preservative in order to reduce the possibility of timber rot. This can be carried out by applying two brush flood coats of preservative.

Storey height frames may be used for internal door openings in thin blockwork partitions. The jambs and head which make up the frame are grooved out on their back face to receive the building blocks. The storey frame should be fixed in position, at the bottom to the wall plate and at the top of the joists, before the blocks are built up (see Figure 5.53). The jambs above the head are cut back to finish flush with the blockwork. As with other frames one jamb should be fixed plumb and the other sighted to it.

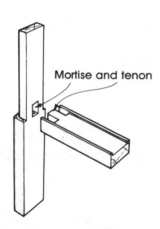

Figure 5.52 Joint detail (storey height frame)

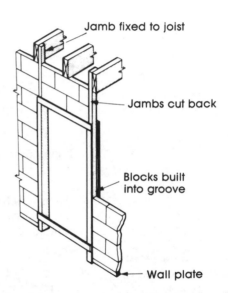

Figure 5.53 'Building in' a storey height frame

'Fixed-in' frames – are sometimes fixed to prepared openings. This applies mainly to expensive hardwood frames and is to protect them from possible damage or discolouration during the building process. In addition, frames that were not available during the building process or replacement frames will have to be 'fixed in'.

Horns on 'fixed-in' frames are not required as a fixing and should be sawn off flush with the back of the jambs. Remember to preservative treat the cut ends.

Place the frame in the prepared opening, temporarily holding it in position with the aid of folding wedges. Check the head or sill for level and adjust the wedges as required.

Plumb one jamb and 'sight in' the other; adjust the wedges if required.

Figure 5.55 shows how to fix the frame to the wall either by:

Nailing using cut nails into the blockwork or brickwork mortar joints or masonry nails into the actual brick.

Screwing plastic plugs and screws through the jamb. Screwheads in softwood frames may be countersunk below the surface and filled. Screwheads in hardwood frames should be concealed by counter boring and pelleting.

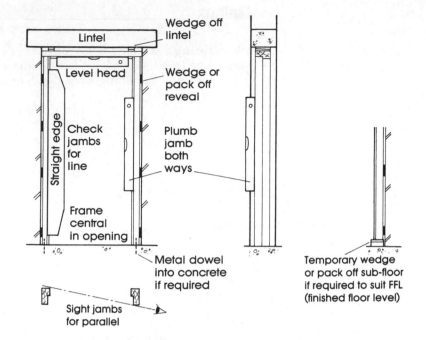

Figure 5.54 Positioning 'fixed-in' frames

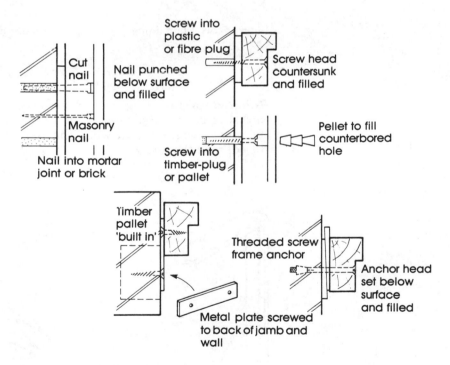

Figure 5.55 Methods of fixing

Metal plates used as fixing lugs screwed at intervals to the back of jamb before the frame is put in the opening. The lugs are screwed and plugged to the brick or block reveals.

Frame anchors – proprietary fixing consisting of a metal or plastic sleeve and matching screw. The jamb and reveal are drilled out to suit the sleeve, which is inserted in position and screwed up tight.

Linings

Plain linings – (Figure 5.56) consist of two plain jambs and a plain head joined together using a bare-faced tongue and housing. The pinned stop is fixed around the lining after the door has been hung.

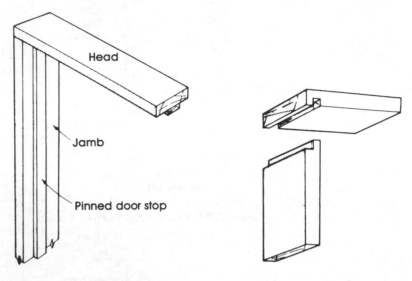

Figure 5.56 Plain lining   **Figure 5.57** Joint detail (plain lining)

Rebated linings – (Figure 5.58) are used for better quality work. They consist of two rebated jambs and a rebated head. The rebate must be the correct width so that when the door is hung it finishes flush with the edges of the lining.

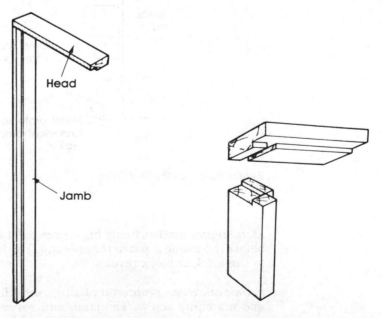

Figure 5.58 Rebated lining   **Figure 5.59** Joint detail (rebated lining)

Fixing linings

The opening in the wall to receive the lining is normally formed while the wall is being built and the lining is fixed at a later stage.

Fixings may be:

Nailing to twisted wooden plugs (see sequence of operations)

Nailing and screwing to timber pallets that have been built into the brick joints by the bricklayer, or into the door stud of a stud partition. Folding wedges are used as packings down the sides of the jambs.

Nailing directly into the blockwork reveal or brickwork mortar joint. Folding wedges will be required as packing.

Using plugs and screws or other proprietary fixing.

Sequence of operations to fix a lining (using twisted timber plugs) as shown in Figure 5.60.
1) Assemble lining. This is normally done by skew nailing through the head into the jambs.
2) Fix a distance piece near the bottom of the jambs, as in Figure 5.60, and when required, diagonal braces at the head.
3) Rake out brickwork joints and plug (see Figure 5.61). There should be at least four fixing points per jamb. Omit this stage if the bricklayer has 'built in' wooden pallets or pads into the brickwork.
4) Offer lining into opening and mark where the plugs need to be trimmed. The plugs should project equally from both reveals.
5) Cut the plugs and check the distance with a width rod. The ends of the plugs should be in vertical alignment. Check with a straight edge and spirit level.

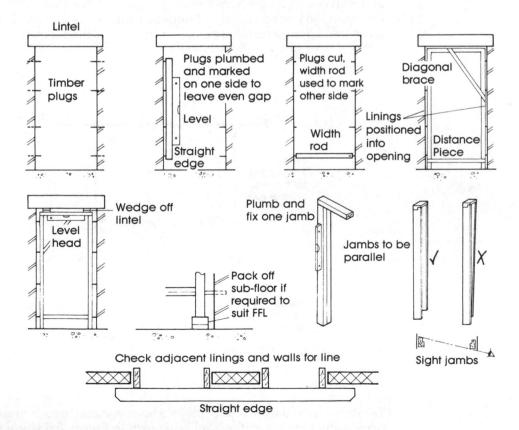

Figure 5.60 Fixing a lining

6) Fix lining plumb and central in the opening by nailing or screwing through the jambs into the plugs. Before finally fixing check head for level, wedge off lintel, ensure the lining is out of wind: check by sighting through the jambs. When fixing to unplastered walls, check adjacent linings and wall surfaces are lined up.

7) Ensure lining jambs are packed up off a concrete sub floor if required to suit the finished floor level (FFL).

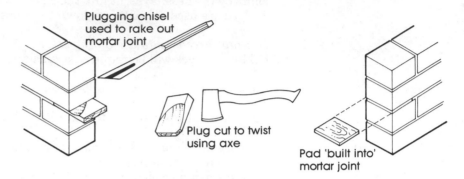

Figure 5.61 Plugs or pads used for fixing lining

Datums

Internal datum – datum positions or lines are often marked around the walls inside a building, particularly in large areas. They should be indicated thus ⊼. The datum line, shown in Figure 5.62, is established at a convenient height, say 1 m above finished floor level (FFL). From this level the position of other building components and finishes can be measured up or down; for example, the heights of floor screed, suspended ceilings, door heads and wall panelling, etc.

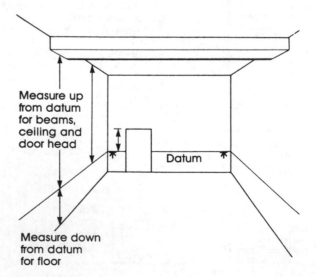

Figure 5.62 Datum line

To establish the datum line, transfer a level position to each corner of the room using either a water level, as shown in Figure 5.63, or a straight edge and spirit level.

Having established the corner positions, stretch a chalk line between each two marks in turn and spring it in the middle, leaving a horizontal chalk dust line on the wall.

Before using a water level it must be prepared by filling it from one end with water, taking care not to trap air bubbles. Check by holding up the two glass tubes side by side: the levels of the water should settle to the same height.

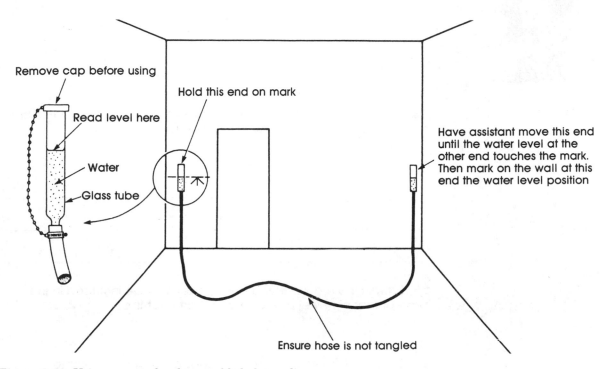

Figure 5.63 Using a water level to establish datum line

Learning task

Refer to the floor plans, range drawing and schedules shown on pp. 189–191.

Determine in metres run the amount of 38 mm × 125 mm and 38 mm × 100 mm required to construct the door linings. Allow 10% for a cutting allowance.

_____

_____

_____

_____

_____

_____

_____ **Questions for you** _____

23. Produce a sketch to show the difference between a door frame and a door lining.

24. Explain the difference between 'built-in' and 'fixed-in' frames and state an occasion where **EACH** might be used.

_____

_____

_____

_____

25. Explain the reason why a steel dowel may be included in the base or foot of newel post and door frame jambs.

_____

26. State the reason why the sawn ends of timber are treated with preservative.

_____

_____

27. Explain how to 'sight in' the jambs of a frame.

_____

_____

28. Explain the purpose of a datum.

_____

_____

29. List **THREE** forms of fixing that can be used to secure frames or linings.

_____

_____

_____

Encasing services

Encasing terminology

Encasing – the casing or boxing in of services. The term casing or boxing, refers to the framework, cladding and trim used to form an enclosure in which service pipes are housed.

Service pipes – the system of pipes for either gas, water or drainage. These are normally fixed within, or on the surface of floors and walls.

Service pipework is cased or boxed in to conceal the pipes thus providing a neat, tidy appearance, which when decorated blends with the main room decoration. In addition they must also provide access to stop valves (stop cocks), drain down valves and cleaning or rodding points.

Encasing guidelines

In many situations encasing services is a simple process of forming an L- or U-shaped box from timber battens, covered with a plywood or hardboard facing. Consider the following simple rules when planning and fixing casings.
- Use standard sections of timber where possible.
- Where casing is to be tiled, ensure the dimensions are simple widths of whole or half tiles.
- Note any stop valve or other fitting which may require access. Fit a separate length of facing board over this section.
- Use WBP (weather and boil proof) plywood or an oil-tempered hardboard for casings in wet areas, e.g. kitchens, bathrooms and laundries, etc.

Battens, typically 32 mm × 32 mm may be fixed to the wall using plugs and screws or nails, cut or masonry, depending on the wall hardness.

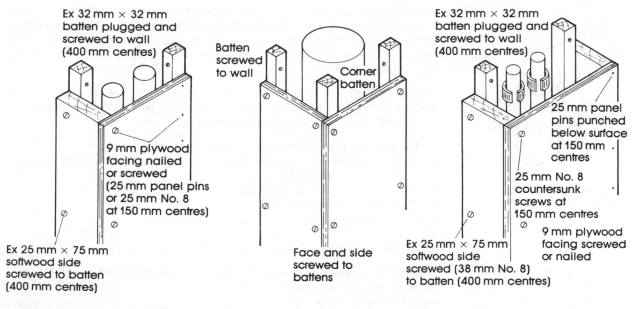

Figure 5.64 Small corner pipe casing

Figure 5.65 Large corner pipe casing

Figure 5.66 Small pipe casing in run of wall

171

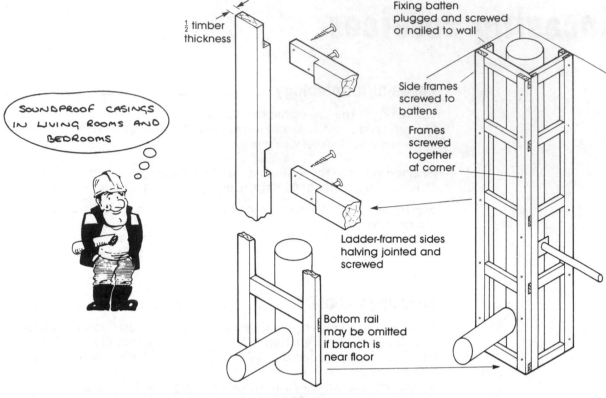

Figure 5.67 Use of ladder frame for pipe casing

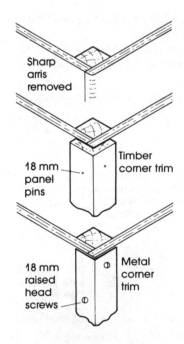

Figure 5.68 Alternative corner treatments

When using 6 mm plywood or 6 mm hardboard, timber ladder frames (see Figure 5.67) are required for support. These are typically 25 mm × 50 mm softwood half lapped together. 9 mm and 12 mm plywood can be used for casing sides direct to battens without a supporting framework. Plywood facing can be nailed or screwed to battens/frames.

Access panels can be screwed in position using brass cups and screws typically 25 mm No. 8. Alternatively they may be hinged as a small door.

Casings have to be scribed to wall surfaces and finished more neatly if they are to be painted or papered rather than tiled. All nails and screws should be punched or sunk below the surface ready for subsequent filling by the painter. The sharp corner arris needs to be removed with glass paper or, as an alternative, may be covered with a timber, metal or plastic trim, as shown in Figure 5.68.

Where casings are located in living rooms or bedrooms they can be packed out with fibreglass, mineral wool or polystyrene in order to quieten the noise of water passing through.

L-shaped casings – are used for pipes in a corner.
● Mark plumb lines on walls. (Use a spirit level and straight edge, as shown in Figure 5.69.)
● Fix battens to the marked lines.
● Fix the side to the batten.
● Fix the front facing to the side and batten.
or
● Make up and fix a ladder frame and fix the facings.

U-shaped casings – are used for pipes in the middle of a wall.
● Mark plumb lines on the wall.
● Fix battens to the marked lines.
● Fix the sides to the battens.
● Fix the front to the sides.

Where pipes branch off the main one, the side will require notching or scribing over them.

For small pipes simply mark the side, drill a hole and saw the side to form a notch as shown in Figure 5.70.

Larger branch pipes are best scribed around with the face split on the pipe's centre line as shown in Figure 5.71.

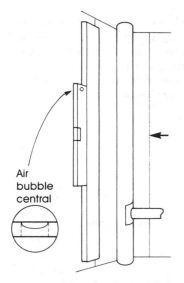

Figure 5.69 Marking plumb line on wall

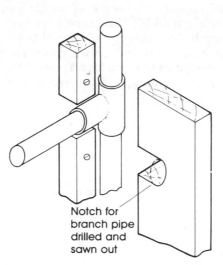

Figure 5.70 Cutting around small branch pipe

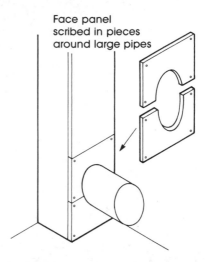

Figure 5.71 Cutting around large branch pipe

Uneven wall surfaces – Sides and faces that fit to an uneven wall surface will require scribing as shown in Figures 5.72–4.
- Position the side against the wall, place a pencil on the wall surface and move it down to mark a parallel line on the side. Plane to the line, slightly undercutting to ensure a tight fit.

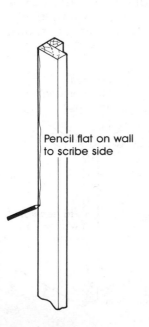

Figure 5.72 Scribing to wall with pencil

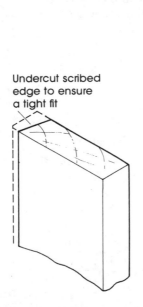

Figure 5.73 Undercutting scribes

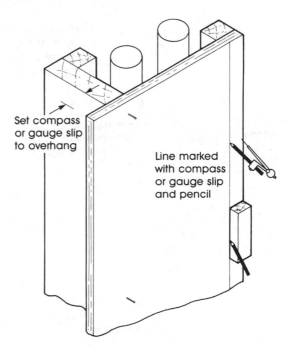

Figure 5.74 Scribing to wall using compass or gauge slip

173

- Cut the ply face oversize (say, 15 mm over required width).
- Position the face against the wall.
- Temporarily nail the face in position, keeping the overhang on the side the same distance from top to bottom.
- Set a compass or gauge slip to the width of overhang. Mark a parallel line on the face.
- Plane or saw to this line, slightly undercutting to ensure a tight fit.

Access panels – the edges of access panels are often chamferred as shown in Figure 5.75. This breaks the straight joint and permits a better paint finish. In addition, removal of the panel is eased without risk of damage. Simply remove screws, run a trimming knife along chamferred joints to cut paint film and lift off panel. Alternatively, access panels may be hinged into a lining and finished with an architrave trim as shown in Figure 5.76.

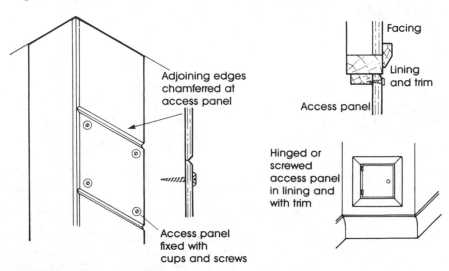

Figure 5.75 Access panel with chamferred edge

Figure 5.76 Access panel in lining

Horizontal pipe casings – are mainly at skirting level. They can be formed using the same construction as vertical casings. Alternatively, they can be formed using a skirting board fixed to a timber top as shown in Figure 5.78.

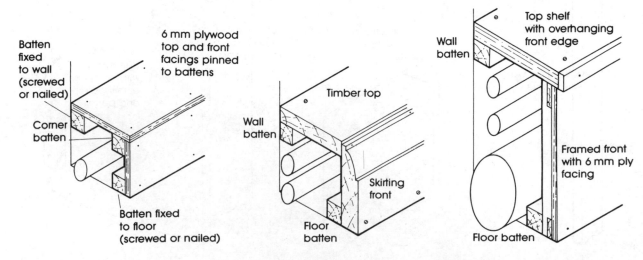

Figure 5.77 Horizontal pipe casing

Figure 5.78 Skirting pipe casing

Figure 5.79 Shelf top to horizontal pipe casing

Taller horizontal casings may have their top extended over the front facing in order to form a useful shelf.
- Mark a level line on the wall. (Use a spirit level and straight edge.)
- Mark a straight line on the floor.
- Fix battens to the marked lines.
- Fix the top and front facing.

Bath front casings

These are termed bath panels. They can be either a standard, normally plastic, set or purpose made.

Standard panels – normally simply fit up under the bath rim and are fixed along their bottom edge to a floor batten as shown in Figure 5.80. Read the specific instructions supplied with the panel for details.

Purpose made panels – have to be fixed (nailed or screwed) to a batten framework as shown in Figure 5.81. This is typically made from ex 25 mm × 50 mm PAR softwood, halved and screwed together.

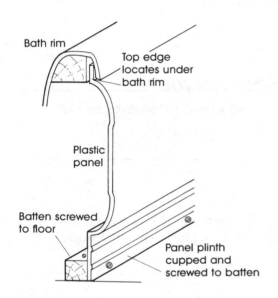

Figure 5.80 Fixing standard bath panel

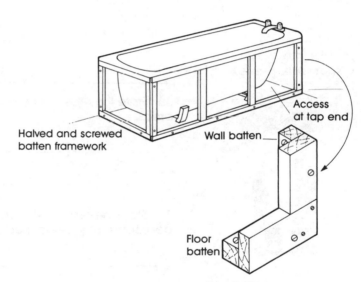

Figure 5.81 Batten framework for a bath panel

The panels can be formed from a variety of materials. For example,
- 9 mm plywood covered with tiles
- 9 mm plywood covered with carpet
- 9 mm veneered plywood with applied mouldings to create a traditional panelled effect
- Matchboarding, TG & V (tongued, grooved and vee jointed)
- 3 mm melamine-faced hardboard

An access panel is often formed at the tap end of the bath for maintenance purposes, rather than removing the whole panel. Figure 5.82 shows how this may be screwed in position or hinged on.
- Ensure the batten framework is set back far enough under the bath rim to allow for the panel thickness (see Figure 5.83).
- Mark plumb lines on the walls.
- Mark a straight line on the floor.
- Fix wall and floor battens to the marked lines.
- Make and fix the battened framework.
- Fix the panel to the framework.

175

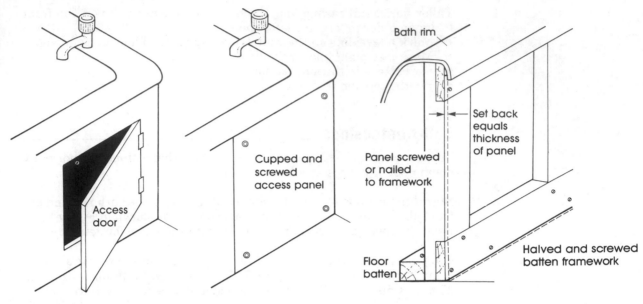

Figure 5.82 Bath access panels

Figure 5.83 Positioning batten framework

TRY TO ANSWER THESE

WELL, HOW DID YOU DO?

WORK THROUGH THE SECTION AGAIN IF YOU HAD ANY PROBLEMS

Questions for you

30. State the reason why WBP plywood is used for casings in wet areas.

31. State the reason why pipe casings located in living rooms or bedrooms may be packed out with fibre glass or mineral wool.

32. State why a removeable access trap may be included in pipe casings.

33. State the purpose of encasing services.

34. Explain why a supporting framework is required when using thin sheet material for pipework casings.

Encasing services

WORD-SQUARE SEARCH

Hidden in the word square are the following 20 words associated with '*Encasing Services*'. You may find the words written forwards, backwards, up, down or diagonally.

Bath	Plywood
Panel	Access
Services	Skirting
Pipe	Softwood
Batten	Halving
Insulation	Plumb
Boxing	Level
Casing	Gauge slip
Scribe	Compass
Notching	Branch pipe

Draw a ring around the words, or line in using a highlight pen thus:

EXAMPLE

EXAMPLE

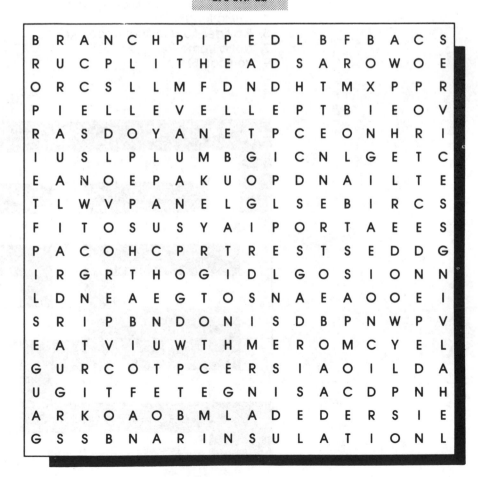

WORD PUZZLE

Solve the clues to complete the word puzzle. All the answers are associated with 'First Fixings'. The number of letters in each word is shown in brackets e.g. (6) indicates a six-letter word and (4) (3) indicates two words having four and three letters each.

Across

2. Regularised studs have a —— width (10)
5. Timber-framed internal wall (4) (9)
6. Lining around stairwell (5)
8. Horizontal measurement of a stair (5)
10. Vertical member fixed at end of string (5)
11. Member cut to fit (7)
12. Used to fill a gap (8)

Down

1. Can be used to help fix a frame (5)
2. Trim to length (3)
3. Stair member that is cut over trimmer (6)
4. Cut to length (3)
5. Provides floor to floor access (6)
7. Not a frame (6)
9. Vertical (5)

6 Second fixings and finishings

READ THIS CHAPTER, WORKING THROUGH THE QUESTIONS AND LEARNING TASKS

In undertaking this chapter you will be required to demonstrate your skill and knowledge of the following second fixing components:
- Doors and ironmongery
- Finishing trim (horizontal and vertical mouldings)
- Kitchen units
- Panelling and cladding

You will be required practically to:
- Hang an external door
- Position and fix mortise lock and letter plate
- Position and fix architraves, skirting and dado rail
- Position and fix floor units, wall units and pre-laminated work top
- Position and fix grounds and vertical matchboard panelling

Doors

REFER TO SOURCES INDICATED FOR FURTHER INFORMATION

Doors may be classified by their method of construction: panelled, glazed, matchboarded, flush, fire resistant, etc., and by their method of operation: swinging, sliding and folding. See *Carpentry and Joinery for Advanced Craft Students: Site Practice* for further information.

Methods of construction

Panelled doors – have a frame made from solid timber rails and stiles, which are jointed using either dowels or mortise and tenon joints. The frame is either grooved or rebated to receive two or more thin plywood or timber panels. Interior doors are thinner than exterior doors.

Glazed doors – are used where more light is required. They are made similar to panelled doors except glass replaces one or more of the plywood or timber panels. Glazing bead is used to secure the glass into its glazing rebates. Glazing bars may be used to divide large glazed areas.

Matchboarded doors – are used mainly externally for gates, sheds and industrial buildings. They are simply constructed from matchboarding, ledges and braces clench nailed together. The bottom end of the braces must always point towards the hanging edge of the door to provide the required support. Framed matchboarded doors constructed with the addition of stiles and rails are used where extra strength is required.

Flush doors – are made with outer faces of plywood or hardboard. Internal doors are normally lightweight having a hollow core, solid tim-

179

ber edges and blocks which are used to reinforce hinge and lock positions. New flush doors will have one edge marked 'LOCK' and the other 'HINGE'; these must be followed. External and fire resistant flush doors are much heavier, as normally they have a solid core of either timber strips or chipboard.

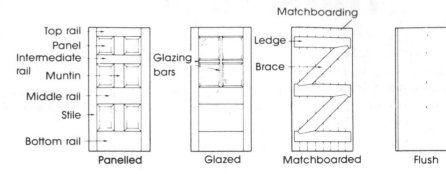

Figure 6.1 Doors

Fire resisting doors – The main function of this type of door is to act as a barrier to a possible fire by providing the same degree of protection as the element in which it is located. They should prevent the passage of smoke, hot gases and flames for a specified period of time. This period of time will vary depending on the relevant statutory regulations and the location of the door.

The fire resistance of a building element and thus the performance of a fire resisting door can be defined by reference to the following criteria:
- Stability: resistance to the collapse of the door
- Integrity: resistance to the passage of flames or hot gases to the unexposed face
- Insulation: resistance to the excessive rise in temperature of the unexposed face

All fire doors can be called 'fire resisting doors', although they should be prefixed by their stability and integrity rating respectively. Thus a 60/45 fire resisting door has a minimum 60 minutes stability rating and a 45 minutes integrity rating.

The more commonly used terms for fire doors are 'fire check' and 'fire resisting'. 'Fire check' is used to signify doors with a reduced integrity.

Table 6.1 Requirements of fire doors

Door type	Stability	Integrity
Half hour fire check	30	20
Half hour fire resisting	30	30
One hour fire check	60	45
One hour fire resisting	60	60

The weak point in fire door construction is the joint between the door and frame. This is where the fire and smoke will penetrate first. Intumescent strips, shown in Figure 6.2, may be fitted around the door opening: when activated by heat in the early stages of a fire these strips expand, sealing the joint and prolonging the door's integrity.

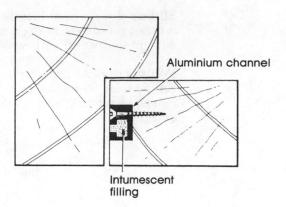

Figure 6.2 Intumescent seal

Door sizes

All mass produced doors may be purchased from a supplier in a range of standard sizes as shown in Figures 6.3 and 6.4. Special sizes or purpose made designs are normally available to order from suppliers with joinery shop contacts.

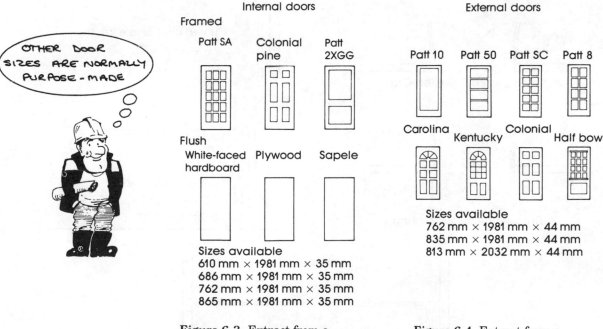

Figure 6.3 Extract from a manufacturer's door list showing range of stock size internal doors

Figure 6.4 Extract from a manufacturer's door list showing range of stock size external doors

Methods of operation

Swinging doors – Side hung on hinges is the most common means of door operation. It is also the most suitable for pedestrian use and the most effective for weather protection, fire resistance, sound and thermal insulation.

Sliding doors – are mainly used either to economise on space where it is not possible to swing a door, or for large openings which would be difficult to close off with swinging doors.

Folding doors – are a combination of swinging and sliding doors. They can be used as either movable internal partitions to divide up large rooms, or alternatively as doors for large warehouses and showroom entrances.

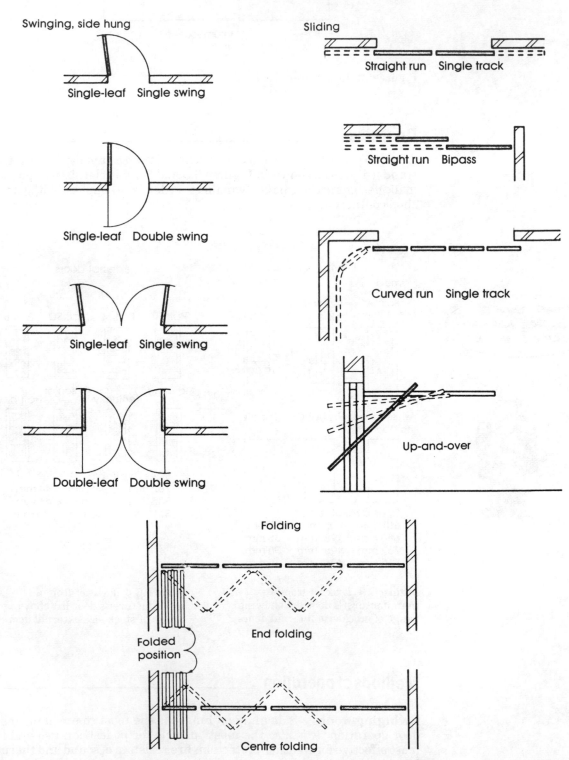

Figure 6.5 Methods of door operation

Door ironmongery

Door ironmongery is also termed door furniture and includes hinges, locks, latches, bolts, other security devices, handles and letter or postal plates. The hand of a door is required in order to select the correct items of ironmongery. Some locks and latches have reversible bolts, enabling either hand to be adapted to suit the situation.

View the door from the hinge knuckle side; if the knuckles are on the left the door is left handed, whereas if the knuckles are on the right, the door is right handed. Figure 6.6 shows how doors may also be defined as either clockwise or anticlockwise closing.

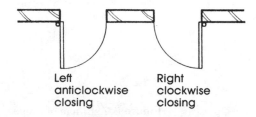

Left
anticlockwise
closing

Right
clockwise
closing

Figure 6.6 Typical handing diagram

Hinges

Hinges are available in a variety of materials: pressed steel are commonly used for internal doors and brass for hardwood and external doors. Do not use steel hinges on hardwood or external doors because of rusting and subsequent staining problems. Do not use nylon, plastic or aluminium hinges on fire-resistant doors because they melt at fairly low temperatures.

Butt hinge – is a general purpose hinge suitable for most applications. As a general rule the leaf with the greatest number of knuckles is fixed to the door frame.

Washered butt hinges – are used for heavier doors, to reduce knuckle wear and prevent squeaking.

Parliament hinges – have wide leaves to extend knuckles and enable doors to fold back against the wall clearing deep architraves, etc.

Rising butts – are designed to lift the door as it opens to clear obstructions such as mats and rugs. They also give a door some degree of self-closing action. In order to prevent the top edge of the door fouling in the frame as it opens and closes, the top edge must be eased as shown in Figure 6.7. The hand of the door must be stated when ordering this item, as they cannot be reversed (i.e. they cannot be altered to suit either hand of door).

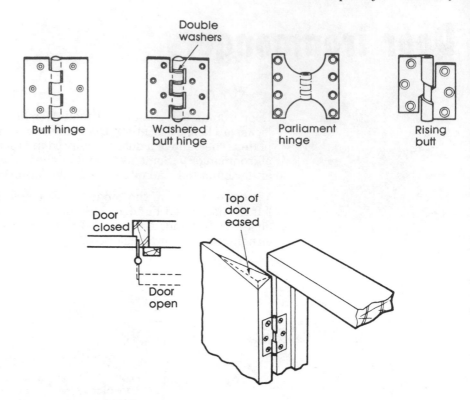

Figure 6.7 Range of hinges

Locks and latches

Cylinder rim latches – are mainly used for entrance doors to domestic property but, as they are only a latch, provide little security on their own. When fitted, the door can be opened from the outside with the use of a key and from the inside by turning the handle. Some types have a double locking facility which improves their security.

Mortise deadlock – provides a straightforward key-operated locking action and is often used to provide additional security on entrance doors where cylinder rim latches are fitted. They are also used on doors where simple security is required, e.g. storerooms.

Mortise latch – is used mainly for internal doors that do not require locking. The latch which holds the door in the closed position can be operated from either side of the door by turning the handle.

Mortise lock/latch – is available in the two types shown in Figure 6.11. The horizontal one is little used nowadays because of its length, which means that it can only be fitted to substantial doors. The vertical type is more modern and can be fitted to most types of doors. It is often known as a narrow-stile lock/latch. Both types can be used for a wide range of general purpose doors in various locations. They are, in essence, a combination of the mortise deadlock and the mortise latch.

Rebated mortise lock/latch – should be used when fixing a lock/latch in double doors that have rebated stiles. The front end of this lock is cranked to fit the rebate on the stiles (see Figure 6.12).

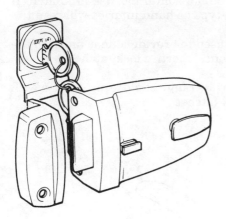

Figure 6.8 Cylinder rim latch

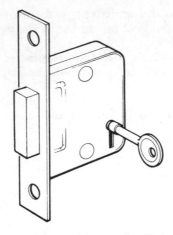

Figure 6.9 Mortise deadlock

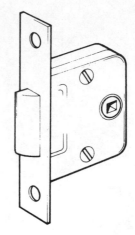

Figure 6.10 Mortise latch

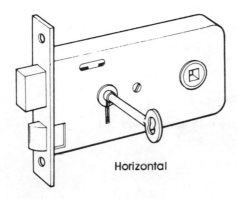

Horizontal

Vertical

Figure 6.11 Mortise lock/latches

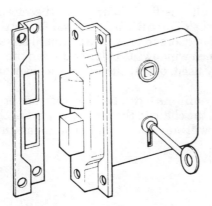

Figure 6.12 Rebated mortise lock/latch

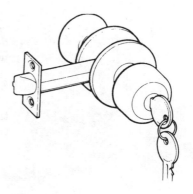

Figure 6.13 Knobset

Knobset – consists of a small mortise latch and a pair of knob handles that can be locked with a key, so that it can be used as a lock/latch in most situations both internally and externally. Knobsets can also be obtained without the lock in the knob for use as a latch only.

Knob furniture – is for use with the horizontal mortise lock/latch. It should not be used with the vertical type as hand injuries will result.

Keyhole escutcheon plates – are used to provide a neat finish to the keyhole of both deadlocks and horizontal mortise lock/latches.

Lever furniture – is available in a wide range of patterns, for use with the mortise latches and mortise lock/latches.

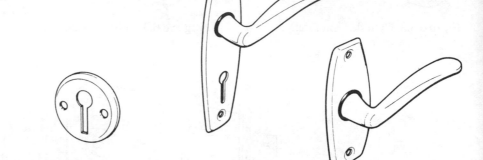

Figure 6.14 Knob furniture   **Figure 6.15** Escutcheon plate   **Figure 6.16** Lever furniture

Barrel bolts – are used on external doors and gates to lock them from the inside. Two bolts are normally used, one at the top of the door and the other at the bottom.

Flush bolt – is flush fitting and therefore requires recessing into the timber (see Figure 6.18). It is used for better quality work on the inside of external doors to provide additional security and also on double doors and French windows to bolt one door in the closed position. Two bolts are normally used, one at the top of the door and the other at the bottom.

Security chains – can be fixed on front entrance doors, the slide to the door and the chain to the frame. When the chain is inserted into the slide, the door will only open a limited amount until the identity of the caller is checked.

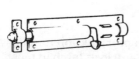

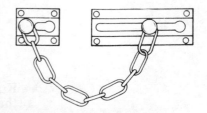

Figure 6.17 Barrel bolt   **Figure 6.18** Flush bolt   **Figure 6.19** Security chain

Ironmongery positioning

Hinge positions – are shown in Figures 6.20 and 6.21. Lightweight internal doors are normally hung on one pair of 75 mm hinges; glazed, half-hour fire resistant and other heavy doors need one pair of 100 mm hinges. All external doors and one-hour fire resistant doors need one and a half pairs of 100 mm hinges. The standard hinge positions for flush doors are 150 mm down from the top, 225 mm up from the bottom and the third hinge where required, positioned centrally. On panelled and glazed doors the hinges are often fixed in line with the rails to produce a more balanced look.

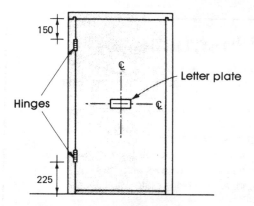

Figure 6.20 Position of hinges and letter plate

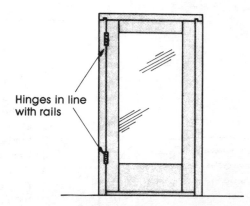

Figure 6.21 Position of hinges on glazed doors

Other furniture positions – will depend on the type of door construction, the specification and the door manufacturer's instructions.

The standard position for mortice locks and latches, shown in Figure 6.22, is 990 mm from the bottom of the door to the centre line of the lever or knob furniture spindle. However, on a panelled door with a middle rail, locks/latches may be positioned centrally in the rail's width. Cylinder rim latches are positioned in the door's style between 1200 mm and 1500 mm from the bottom of the door and the centre line of the cylinder. Before fitting any locks/latches the width of the door stile should be measured to ensure the lock/latch length is shorter than the stile's

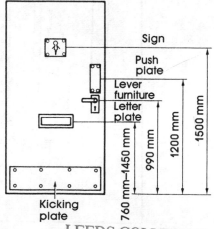

Figure 6.22 Fixing heights

width, otherwise a narrow stile lock may be required. Letter plates are normally positioned centrally in a door's width and between 760 mm and 1450 mm from the bottom of the door to the centre line of the plate. Again on panelled doors letter plates may be positioned centrally in a rail and sometimes even vertically in a stile.

Always read the job specification as exact furniture positions may be stated.

Always read both the door manufacturer's instructions and the ironmongery manufacturer's instructions to ensure the intended position is suitable to receive the item, e.g. the positioning of the lock block on a flush door, and the item is fixed correctly.

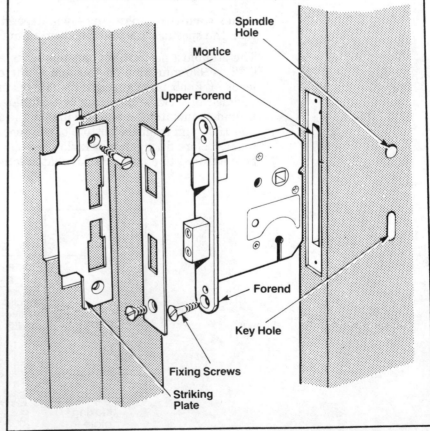

Fixing Instructions

1. At the desired height drill a 15mm ($^{19}/_{32}''$) diameter spindle hole at a distance of 44mm ($1^3/_4''$) from the edge of the door. 57mm ($2^1/_4''$) for 3″.
2. At the position of the key hole cut away a section to suit, in line with the spindle hole.
3. Mortice door for lock case and forend.
4. Remove upper forend by removing small lug screws.
5. Fit mortice lock and secure with screws provided.
6. Replace upper forend. Align striking plate with lock and mortice frame to suit.
7. Fix striking plate with two wood screws.

NOTE:
The bolt is reversible. Simply remove lock case, remove latch mechanism, reverse and replace.

Figure 6.23 Typical manufacturer's fixing instructions

Door and ironmongery schedules

Schedules are used to record repetitive design information. Read with a range drawing and floor plans, they may be used to identify a type of door, its size, the number required, the door opening in which it fits, the hinges it will swing on and details of other furniture to be fitted to it.

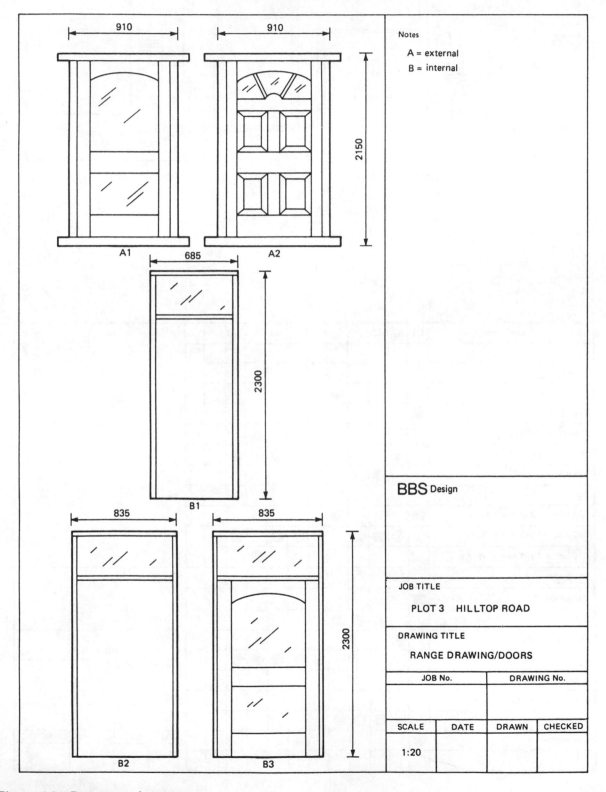

Notes

A = external

B = internal

BBS Design

JOB TITLE

PLOT 3   HILLTOP ROAD

DRAWING TITLE

RANGE DRAWING/DOORS

JOB No.		DRAWING No.	
SCALE	DATE	DRAWN	CHECKED
1:20			

Figure 6.24 Door range drawing

6 Second fixings and finishings

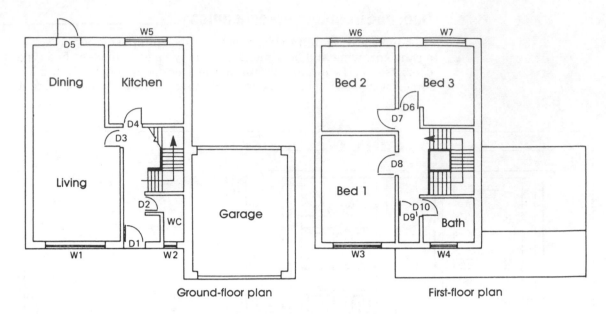

Figure 6.25 Floor plans

Description	D1	D2	D3	D4	D5	D6	D7	D8	D9	D10			NOTES
Type (see range)													
External glazed A1					●								
External panelled A2	●												
Internal flush B1									●				
Internal flush B2		●				●	●	●		●			
Internal glazed B3			●	●									
Size													
813 mm × 2032 mm × 44 mm	●				●								
762 mm × 1981 mm × 35 mm		●	●	●		●	●	●		●			
610 mm × 1981 mm × 35 mm									●				
Material													BBS DESIGN
Hardwood	●												
Softwood			●	●	●								
Plywood/polished		●											JOB TITLE
plywood/painted						●	●	●	●	●			PLOT 3 Hilltop Road
Infill													DRAWING TITLE
6 mm tempered safety glass													Door Schedule/doors
clear			●	●	●								JOB NO. DRAWING NO.
obscured	●												
													SCALE DATE DRAWN CHECKED

190   **Figure 6.26** Door schedules

Door ironmongery

Description	D1	D2	D3	D4	D5	D6	D7	D8	D9	D10		NOTES
Frames												
75 mm × 100 mm (outward opening)					●							
75 mm × 100 mm (inward opening)	●											
Linings												
38 mm × 125 mm		●	●	●								
38 mm × 100 mm						●	●	●	●	●		
Shape												
Rebated stop	●				●							
Planted stop		●	●	●		●	●	●	●	●		
Transom		●	●	●		●	●	●	●	●		BBS DESIGN
Sill	●				●							
Material												
Hardwood	●											
Softwood		●	●	●	●	●	●	●	●	●		JOB TITLE PLOT 3 Hilltop Road
Fanlight infill												DRAWING TITLE Door Schedule/frames/lining
6 mm tempered safety glass												JOB NO. / DRAWING NO.
clear												
obscured		●							●			
6 mm plywood									●			SCALE / DATE / DRAWN / CHECKED

Figure 6.26 Door schedules – continued

Description	D1	D2	D3	D4	D5	D6	D7	D8	D9	D10		NOTES
Hanging												
Pair 100 mm pressed steel butt hinges			●	●	●[1.5]							
Pair 100 mm brass butt hinges	●[1.5]											
Pair 75 mm pressed steel butt hinges						●	●	●	●[1.5]	●		
Pair 75 mm brass butt hinges		●										
Fastening												
Rim night latch	●											
Mortise deadlock	●											
Mortise lock/latch		●			●				●			
Mortise latch			●	●		●	●	●				
100 mm brass bolts	●[2]				●[2]							BBS DESIGN
Miscellaneous												
Brass lock/latch furniture		●			●				●			
Brass latch furniture			●	●		●	●	●				JOB TITLE PLOT 3 Hilltop Road
Brass letterplate	●											DRAWING TITLE Ironmongery schedule/doors
Brass knocker	●											
Brass coat hook		●[2]							●[2]			JOB NO. / DRAWING NO.
Brass escutcheon	●[2]											
												SCALE / DATE / DRAWN / CHECKED

Figure 6.26 Door schedules – continued

Details relevant to a particular door opening are indicated in the schedules by a dot or cross, a figure is also included where more than one item is required. Extracting details from a schedule is called 'taking off'. The following information concerning the WC door D2 has been taken off the schedules.

One polished plywood internal flush door type B2 762 mm × 1981 mm × 35 mm, hung on one pair of 75 mm brass butts and fitted with one mortice lock/latch, one brass mortice lock/latch furniture and two brass coat hooks.

READ THE INSTRUCTIONS AND COMPLETE THE TASK

Learning task

Take off the following information from the schedules.
How many type B2 painted doors are required?

_____

Produce a list of hinges required for the whole house.

_____

_____

_____

_____

State the size and type of door for opening D1.

_____

_____

Door hanging

Door hanging is normally carried out before skirtings and architraves are fixed. Speed and confidence in door hanging can be achieved by following the procedure illustrated in Figure 6.27 and outlined below:
1) Measure height and width of door opening.
2) Locate and mark the top and hanging side of the opening and door.
   Note: On flush and fire-check doors these should have been marked by the manufacturer.
   When the hanging side is not shown on the drawing, the door should open into the room to provide maximum privacy, but not onto a light switch.
3) Cut off the horns (protective extensions on the top and bottom of each stile) on panelled doors. Flush doors will probably have protective pieces of timber or plastic on each corner, these need to be prised off.
4) 'Shoot' (plane to fit) in the hanging stile of door to fit the hanging side of the opening. A leading edge will be required to prevent binding.

5) 'Shoot' the door to width. Allow a 2 mm joint all around between door and frame or lining. Many carpenters use a two pence coin to check. The closing side will require planing to a slight angle to allow it to close.
6) 'Shoot' the top of the door to fit the head of the opening. Saw or shoot the bottom of the door to give a 6 mm gap at floor level or to fit the threshold.
7) Mark out and cut in the hinges. Screw one leaf of each hinge to the door.
8) Offer up the door to the opening and screw the other leaf of each hinge to the frame.

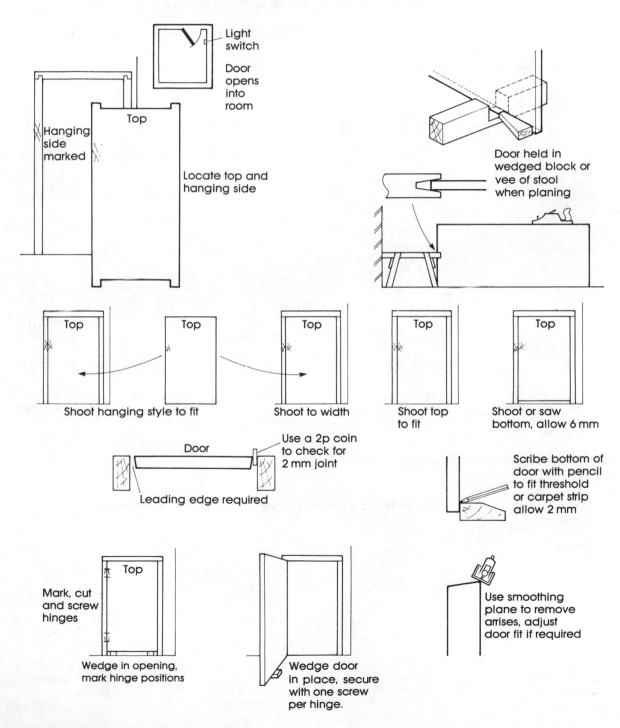

Figure 6.27 Typical door hanging procedure

9) Adjust fit as required. Remove all arrises (sharp edges) to soften the corners and provide a better surface for the subsequent paint finish. If the closing edge rubs the frame, the hinges may be proud and require the recesses being cut deeper. If the recesses are too deep, the door will not close fully and tend to spring open, which is known as 'hinge bound'. In this case a thin cardboard strip can be placed in the recess to pack out the hinge.

10) Fit and fix the lock.

11) Fit any other ironmongery, e.g. bolts, letter plates, handles, etc.

It is usual practice to only fit and not to fix the other ironmongery, e.g. handles and bolts, etc., at this stage. They should be fixed later during the finishing stage after all painting works are completed.

Mortice dead lock – fitting procedure is shown in Figure 6.28.

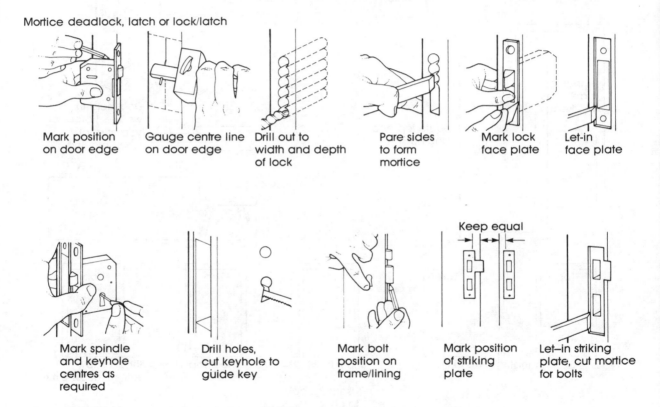

Figure 6.28 Fitting procedure for locks and latches

Cylinder rim – fitting procedure is shown in Figure 6.29.

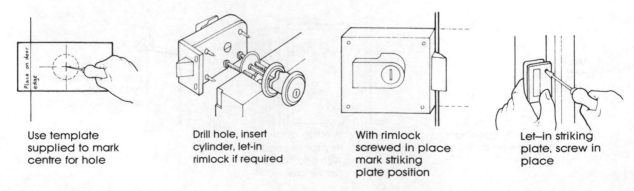

Figure 6.29 Fitting procedure for a cylinder rim night latch

Letter plate – fitting procedure is shown in Figure 6.30.

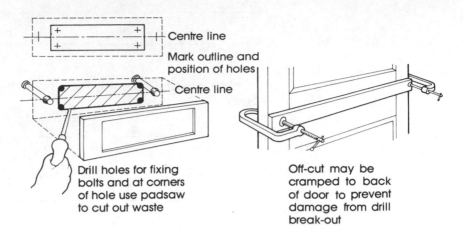

Figure 6.30 Fitting procedure for a letter plate

Questions for you

1. State the purpose of door and ironmongery schedules.

_____

_____

2. Produce a sketch to show the typical positions of the hinges and mortise lock/latch to an external plywood flush door.

3. State why manufacturer's instructions should be followed when fitting ironmongery.

_____

_____

4. State the purpose of a leading edge to door stiles.

_____

_____

5. Define arris and state why they should be removed from door edges.

_____

_____

_____

6. Explain the treatment required to the top edge of a door head when hung using rising butts.

_____

_____

7. State why the stile of a door should be measured before ordering any ironmongery.

_____

_____

8. List the sequence of operations for hanging an external front door to a domestic property.

_____

_____

_____

_____

_____

_____

WELL, HOW DID YOU DO?

WORK THROUGH THE SECTION AGAIN IF YOU HAD ANY PROBLEMS

Door ironmongery

WORD-SQUARE SEARCH

Hidden in the word square are the following 20 words associated with '*Doors and door ironmongery*'. You may find the words written forwards, backwards, up, down or diagonally.

Door	Mortise
External	Cylinder
Panelled	Knobset
Flush	Lever
Folding	Security
Knuckle	Bolt
Hinge	Letter
Lock	Schedule
Latch	Hanging
Hand	Shoot

Draw a ring around the words, or line in using a highlight pen thus:

EXAMPLE

EXAMPLE

```
E X T E R N A L F K D E L L E N A P
E G H F F G H J M N O Q S U W Y A B
H S U L F E I K M H P R T V X Z C T
C A C E O F K G B E I G I K N H O E
T B R H L T G J C F H N J M L A P S
A C E K D E N C F G K D G A G N E B
L A V G I E I K J I O H G E F D C O
C B E C N I G Z X O Y C O P E D I N
Y B L I G N N G R O S S L O W E D K
T D O O K C A S E F I R O O D O G O
I C I H E R H I A C O M C I C B E R
R O E A M O R L A Y H O K K O T X E
U B A C O B R T S L C O V E L R O T
C A H T R S F E G I E D A O L E M T
E C I M T X Y Z A N A M B K T L H E
S F J O I R P Q S D G N C F U O Y L
B G K P S W T U V E H O E V O L I E
E L U D E H C S E R M K N U C K L E
```

Finishing trim

Vertical and horizontal mouldings

These are often referred to as trim and include architraves, skirting, dado rail, picture rail and cornice. They are used to cover the joint between adjacent surfaces, such as wall and floor/ceiling or the joint between plaster and frames. In addition they provide a decorative feature, and may also serve to protect the wall surface from knocks.

Vertical – a line at right angles to the skyline. It is perpendicular to the horizon or horizontal.

Horizontal – a plane or line lying from side to side, parallel with the skyline as opposed to vertical which is up and down at right angles to the horizontal.

Architrave – the decorative trim that is placed internally around door and window openings to mask the joint between wall and timber and conceal any subsequent shrinkage and expansion.

Skirting – the horizontal trim, often a timber board, that is fixed around the base of a wall to mask the joint between the wall and floor (see Figure 6.32). It also protects the plaster surface from knocks at low level.

Dado rail – a moulding applied to the lower part of interior walls at about waist height approximately 1 m from the floor. It is also known as a chair rail as it coincides with a tall chair back height to protect the plaster.

Picture rail – a moulding applied to the upper part of interior walls between 1.8 m and 2.1 m from the floor. Special clips are hooked over the rail in order to suspend the picture frames.

Cornice – the moulding used internally at the wall/ceiling junction. It is normally formed from plaster, only rarely from timber.

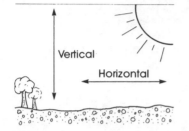

Figure 6.31 Vertical is up and down, horizontal is side to side

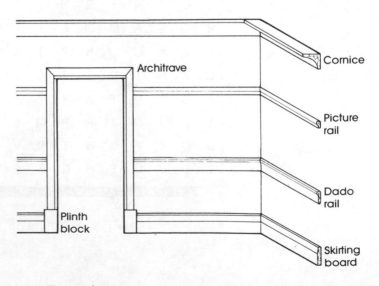

Figure 6.32 Types of trim

Trim – the collective term for vertical and horizontal mouldings. They are normally ready to assemble, machined to a range of standard profiles (shapes) as shown in Figure 6.33.

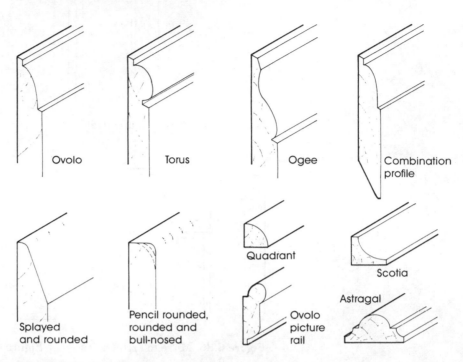

Ovolo   Torus   Ogee   Combination profile

Splayed and rounded   Pencil rounded, rounded and bull-nosed   Quadrant   Ovolo picture rail   Scotia   Astragal

Figure 6.33 Standard trim sections

Skirting is often mass produced using a combination profile, e.g. with an ovolo mould on one face and edge and a splayed and rounded on the other. This enables it to be used for either purpose and also reduces the timber merchant's stock range. In addition the moulding profile has the effect of an undercut edge enabling it to fit snugly to the floor surface.

Cutting and fixing trim

Solid timber either softwood or hardwood is used for the majority of mouldings. However, MDF (medium density fibreboard) and low density foamed core plastics are used to a limited extent for moulding production.

The following cutting and fixing details are generally suitable for all three of these materials. Consult manufacturer's instructions prior to starting to fix other proprietary mouldings/trim.

Architraves – Figure 6.34 shows that a set of architraves consist of a horizontal head and two vertical jambs or legs.

A 6 mm to 9 mm margin is normally left between the frame or lining edge and the architrave. This margin provides a neat appearance to an opening; an unsightly joint line would result if architraves were to be kept flush with the edge of the opening.

The return corners of a set of architraves are mitred. For right-angled returns (90 degrees) the mitre will be 45 degrees (half the total angle) and can be cut using a mitre box or block as shown in Figure 6.37.

Mitres for corners other than right angles will be half the angle of intersection. They can be practically found by marking the outline of

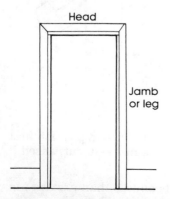

Head

Jamb or leg

Figure 6.34 Architraves

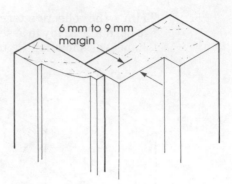

Figure 6.35 Margin to architraves

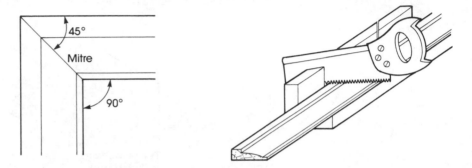

Figure 6.36 Mitre to architraves   **Figure 6.37** Cutting mitre

the intersecting trim on the frame/lining or wall, and joining the inside and outside corners to give the mitre line (see Figure 6.38). Moulding can be marked directly from this or alternatively an adjustable bevel can be set up for use.

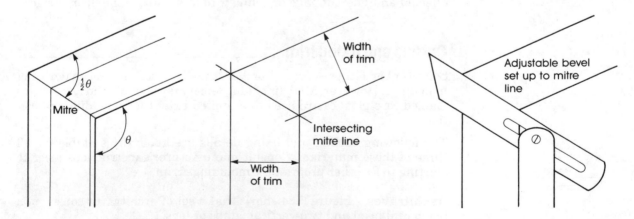

Figure 6.38 Determining mitre for corners other than right angles

The head is normally marked, cut and temporarily fixed in position first as shown in Figure 6.39. The jambs can then be marked, cut, eased if required and subsequently fixed.

Where the corner is not square or you have been less than accurate in cutting the mitre, it will require easing, either with a block plane or by running a tenon saw through the mitre.

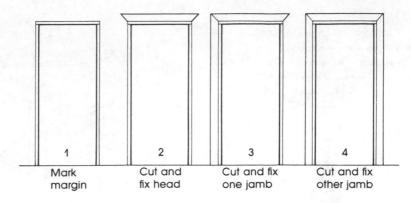

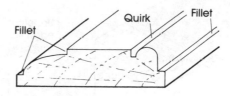

Figure 6.39 Marking and fixing architraves

Fixing is normally direct to the door frame/lining at between 200 mm and 300 mm centres using typically 38 mm or 50 mm long oval or lost-head nails. These should be positioned in the fillets or quirks (flat surface or groove in moulding, see Figure 6.41) and punched in.

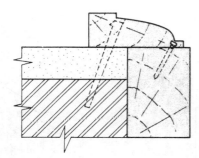

Figure 6.40 Normal method of fixing architraves

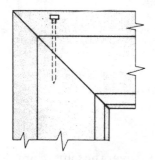

Figure 6.41 Fixings best positioned in fillets or quirks for concealment

Mitres should be nailed through their top edge to reinforce the joint and ensure both faces are kept flush (see Figure 6.42). 38 mm oval or lost-head nails are suitable for this purpose.

In addition architraves, especially very wide ones, are often fixed back to the wall surface using either cut or masonry nails. (Do not forget eye protection.)

A *plinth block* is a block of timber traditionally fixed at the base of an architrave to take the knocks and abrasions at floor level (see Figure 6.43). It is also used to ease fixing problems which occur when skirtings are thicker than the architrave.

In current practice plinth blocks will rarely be found except in restoration work, new high quality work in traditional style or where the skirting is thicker than the architrave.

Architraves may be butt jointed to the plinth block, but traditionally they were joined using bare-faced tenon and screws.

Architraves should be scribed (one member cut to fit over the contour of another) to fit the wall surface, where frames/linings abut a wall at right angles.

Figure 6.42 Nailing mitre joints at corners of architraves

- Temporarily fix the architrave jamb in position, keeping the over-hang the same all the way down. Figure 6.44 shows how to set a

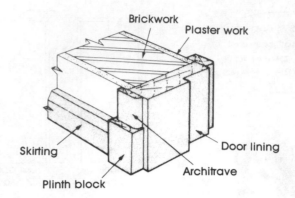

Figure 6.43 Use of plinth blocks

compass to the required margin plus the overhang, or alternatively use a piece of timber this size (gauge block).

● Mark with the compass or gauge slip the line to be cut.
● By slightly undercutting the edge (making it less than 90 degrees) it will fit snugly to the wall contour as shown in Figure 6.45.

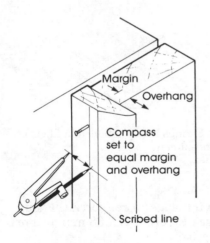

Figure 6.44 Scribing architraves

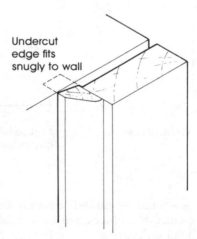

Figure 6.45 Scribe should fit snugly to wall surface

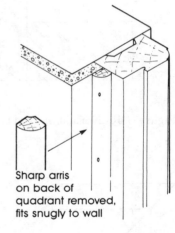

Figure 6.46 Use of quadrants as an alternative to scribing

A quadrant mould or scotia mould are often used to cover the joint to provide a neat finish to the reveal of external door frames. Quadrant moulds may also be used in place of an architrave jamb where the frame/lining join to a wall at right angles. The sharp arris on the quadrant mould is best parred off with a chisel, as shown in Figure 6.46, to enable the mould to sit snugly into the plaster/timber intersection.

All nails used for fixings should be punched below the surface on completion of the work. This is in preparation for subsequent filling by the painter.

Skirting – this is normally cut and fixed directly after the architrave.

Internal corners of 90 degrees and less (right angles and acute angles) are scribed, one piece being cut to fit over the other.

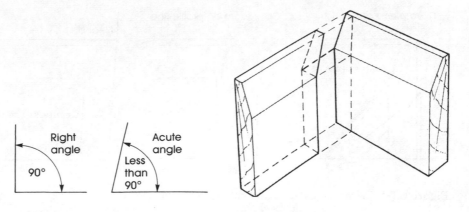

Figure 6.47 Internal corners 90° or less

Figure 6.48 Scribing internal corners

Scribes can be formed in one of two ways:

Mitre and scribe – Fix one piece and cut an internal mitre on the other piece to bring out the profile as shown in Figure 6.49. Cut the profile square on mitre line to remove waste. Use a coping saw for the curve.

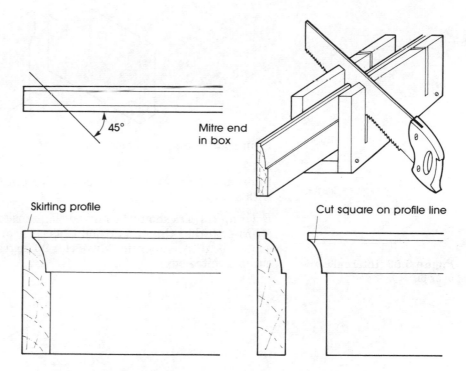

Figure 6.49 Cutting an internal scribe (mitre and scribe)

Compass scribe – Fix one piece, place other piece in position. Scribe with a compass as shown in Figure 6.50. Cut square on the scribed line to remove waste.

Scribing is the preferred method, especially where the walls are slightly out of plumb. The mitred scribe would have a gap, but the compass scribe would fit the profile neatly.

6 Second fixings and finishings

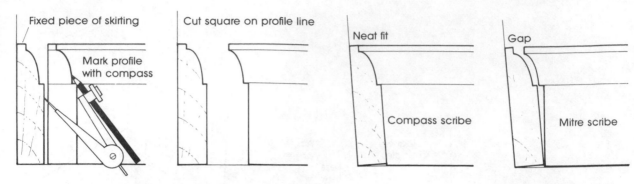

Figure 6.50 Compass marking and cutting a scribe

Mitres are not normally used for internal corners of skirting. Wall corners are rarely perfectly square, making the fitting difficult. In addition mitres open up as a result of shrinkage, forming a much larger gap than scribes.

However, internal corners on bullnosed or pencil rounded skirtings may be cut with a false or partial mitre on the top rounded edge and the remaining flat surface scribed to fit as shown in Figure 6.51.

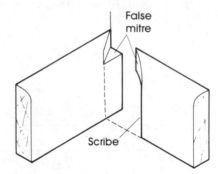

Figure 6.51 False mitre and scribe

Figure 6.52 Internal corner over 90°

Internal corners over 90 degrees, called obtuse angles, are best jointed with a mitre.

External corners should be mitred. These return the moulding profile at a corner rather than a butt joint, as seen in Figure 6.54, which would show unsightly end grain. Mitres for 90 degree external corners may be cut in a mitre box.

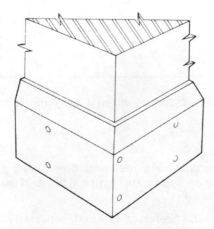

Figure 6.53 Mitring external corners

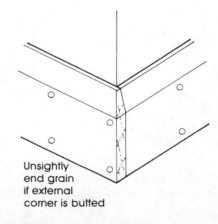

Figure 6.54 Butting of external corners not recommended

Mitres for both internal and external corners over 90 degrees can be marked out using the following method, illustrated in Figures 6.55–7, and then cut freehand.

1) Use a piece of skirting to mark line and width of skirting on floor either side of the mitre.

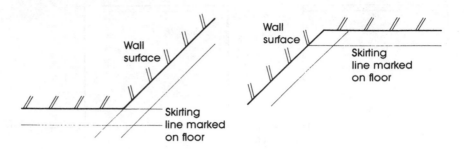

Figure 6.55 Line of skirting for corners over 90°

2) Place length of skirting in position.
3) Mark position of plaster arris on top edge of skirting. For internal corners this will be the actual back edge of the skirting.
4) Mark outer section on front face of skirting.
5) Use try square to mark line across face and back surface of skirting.
6) Cut mitre freehand.
7) Repeat marking out and cutting procedure for other piece.
8) Fix skirting to wall, external corners should be nailed through the mitre.

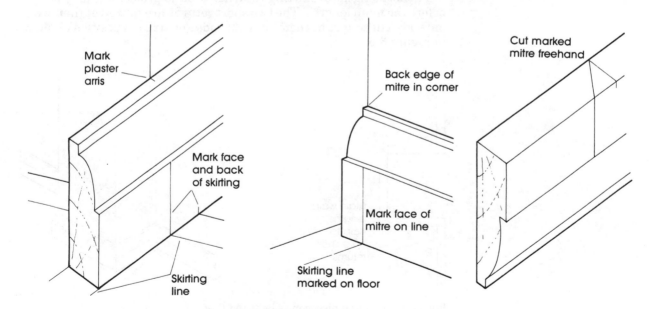

Figure 6.56 Marking out external corners over 90°   **Figure 6.57** Marking out internal corners over 90°

Long lengths are fixed first as indicated in Figure 6.58, starting with those having two trapped ends (both ends between walls). Marking and jointing internal corners is much easier when one end is free.

Where the second piece to be fixed also has two trapped ends, a piece slightly longer than the actual length required, by say 50 mm, can be

205

angled across the room or allowed to run through the door opening for scribing the internal joint.

After scribing and cutting to length it can be fixed in position.

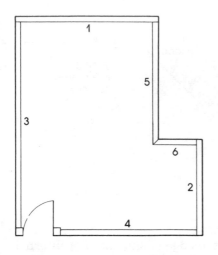

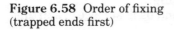

Figure 6.58 Order of fixing (trapped ends first)

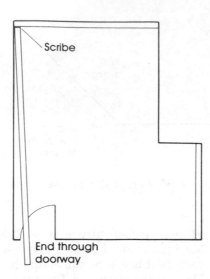

Figure 6.59 Extend through doorway to permit scribing of joint

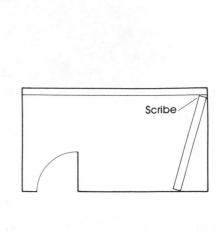

Figure 6.60 Angle and scribe when second piece has both ends trapped

Very short lengths of skirting returned around projections may be fixed before the main lengths. The two short returns are mitred at their external ends, cut square at their internal ends and fixed in position as shown in Figure 6.61.

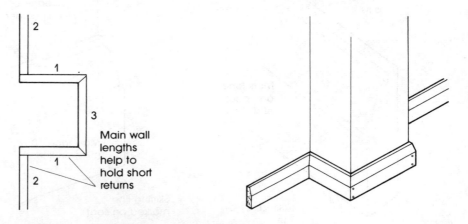

Figure 6.61 Small pieces may be fitted first

Main wall lengths are scribed and fixed in position. These help to hold the short returns. Finally the front piece is cut and fixed in position by nailing through the mitres.

Heading joints can be used where sufficiently long lengths of skirting are not available. Mitres are preferred to butts, because the two surfaces are held flush together by nailing through the mitre (see Figure 6.62). In addition mitres mask any gap appearing as a result of shrinkage.

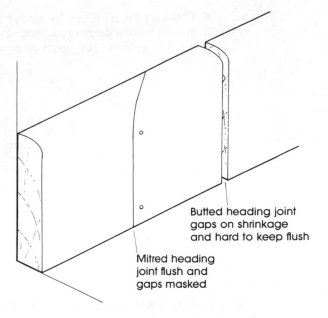

Figure 6.62 Mitres are preferred for heading joints

Where skirtings and other trim is to be fixed around a curved surface, the back face will almost certainly require *kerfing*. This involves putting saw cuts in the back face at regular intervals to effectively reduce the thickness of the trim. This is shown in Figures 6.63 and 6.64. The kerfs, which may be cut with a tenon saw, should be spaced between 25 mm and 50 mm apart. The tighter the curve, the closer together the kerfs should be. The depth of the kerfs must be kept the same. They should extend through the section to the maximum extent, but just keeping back from the face and top edge.

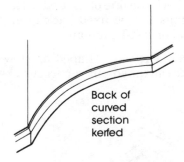

Figure 6.63 Fixing to a curved surface

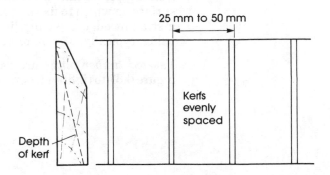

Figure 6.64 Kerfing to the back of a skirting board

Care is required when fixing trim back to the wall, to ensure that it is bent gradually and evenly. It is at this time that accuracy in cutting the kerfs evenly spaced to a constant depth is rewarded. Any overcutting and the trim is likely to snap at that point.

Mitres at the ends of curved sections may be marked out and cut using the same methods as described for other obtuse angles.

Skirtings and other mouldings may occasionally be required to stop part way along a wall, rather than finish into a corner or another moulding. In these circumstances the profile should be returned to the wall or floor.

207

This can be achieved by either mitring the end and inserting a short mitred return piece or, alternatively, the return profile can be cut across the end grain of the main piece as shown in Figure 6.65.

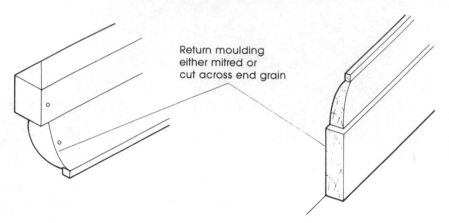

Figure 6.65 Return the profile of moulding that stops part way along a wall

Fixing – Skirting can be fixed back to walls with the aid of:
- grounds
- timber twisted plugs
- direct to the surface

Grounds are timber battens which are fixed to the wall surface using either cut nails in mortar joints or masonry nails (see Figure 6.66). One ground is required for skirtings up to 100 mm in depth. Deeper skirtings require either the addition of vertical soldier grounds at 400 mm to 600 mm centres or an extra horizontal ground. The top ground should be fixed about 10 mm below the top edge of the skirting.

Packing pieces may be required behind the grounds to provide a true surface on which to fix the skirting. Check the line of ground with either a straight edge or string line. Skirtings can be fixed back to grounds using, typically, 38 mm or 50 mm oval or lost-head nails.

Twisted timber plugs are rarely used. They are shaped as shown in Figure 6.67 to tighten when driven into the raked-out vertical brickwork

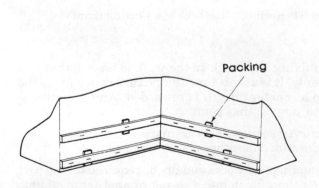

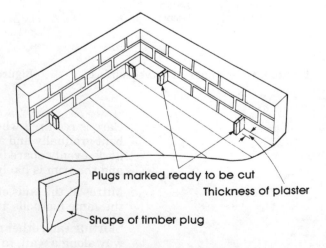

Packing

Plugs marked ready to be cut

Thickness of plaster

Shape of timber plug

Figure 6.66 Fixing skirting to timber grounds   **Fixing 6.67** Fixing skirting to timber plugs

joints at approximately 600 mm apart. When all the plugs have been fixed, they should be cut off to provide a true line. An allowance should be made for the thickness of the plaster.

Skirtings can be fixed back into the end grain of the plugs using, typically, 50 mm cut nails. These hold better in the end grain than would oval or lost-head nails.

Prior to fixing mouldings across any wall, a check should be made to see if any services are hidden below the wall surface. Fixing into electric cables and gas or water pipes is potentially dangerous and expensive to repair. Wires to power points normally run vertically up from the floor. Wires to light switches normally run vertically down from the ceiling. Therefore keep clear of these areas when fixing. Buried pipes in walls are harder to spot. Vertical pipes may just be seen at floor level; outlet points may also be visible (see Figure 6.68). Assume both of these run the full height of the wall, both up and down. Therefore, again keep clear of these areas when fixing. When in doubt an electronic device can be used to scan the wall surface prior to fixing. This gives off a loud noise when passing over buried pipes and electric cables.

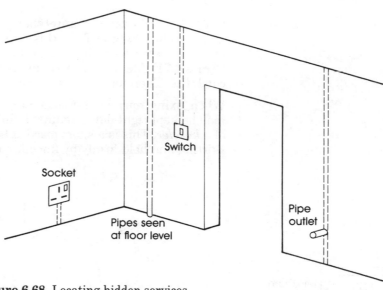

Figure 6.68 Locating hidden services

Direct to the wall. Skirtings are fixed back to the wall after plastering, using typically either 50 mm cut nails or 50 mm masonry nails depending on the hardness of the wall. Oval or lost-head nails may be used to fix skirtings to timber studwork partitions.

Figure 6.69 shows that fixings should be spaced at 400 mm to 600 mm centres. These should be double nailed near the top and bottom edge of the skirting or alternatively they may be staggered between the top and bottom edge. Remember all nails should be punched below the surface.

Hardwood skirtings for very high quality work may be screwed in position. These should either be counterbored and filled with cross-grained pellets on completion, or brass screws and cups as shown in Figure 6.70 should be used.

The Building Regulations 1985 AD:J restricts the use of combustible materials (including timber) around heat-producing appliances and their flues. In general no structural timber (joists and rafters) is to be built into a flue, or be within 200 mm of the flue lining, or nearer than 40 mm to the outer surface of a flue.

209

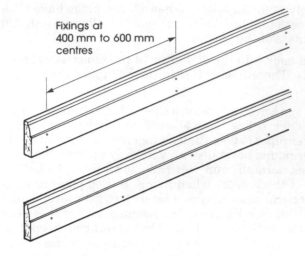

Fixings at 400 mm to 600 mm centres

Figure 6.69 Spacing of fixings

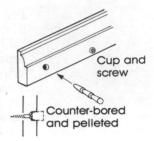

Cup and screw

Counter-bored and pelleted

Figure 6.70 Screws sometimes used to fix hardwood skirtings

Skirtings, architraves, mantel shelves and other trim are non-structural and therefore exempt from this requirement. However, any metal fixings associated with these must be at least 50 mm from the flue (see Figure 6.71). Metal rapidly conducts heat which could cause the trim to catch fire. Therefore, do not use overlong fixings in this situation.

When fixing narrow skirtings, say 75 mm to 100 mm in depth, they may be kept tight down against a fairly level floor surface with the aid of a *kneeler*. This is a short piece of board placed on the top edge of the skirting and held firmly by kneeling on it as shown in Figure 6.72.

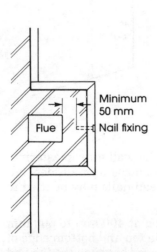

Minimum 50 mm

Flue — Nail fixing

Figure 6.71 Fixings near flues

Figure 6.72 Keeping skirting tight to floor surface when fixing

Deeper skirtings and/or uneven floor surfaces may require scribing to close the gaps before fixing. This is carried out if required, after jointing but prior to fixing.
1) Place cut length of skirting in position.
2) Use gauge slip or compass set to widest gap to mark on the skirting a line parallel to the uneven surface as shown in Figure 6.73.
3) Trim skirting to line using either a handsaw or plane.
4) Undercut the back edge to ensure the front edge snugly fits the floor contour (see Figure 6.74).

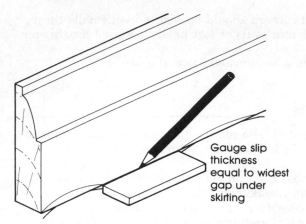

Figure 6.73 Scribing skirting to an uneven floor surface

Gauge slip thickness equal to widest gap under skirting

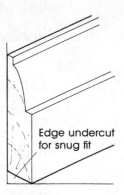

Edge undercut for snug fit

Figure 6.74 Bottom edge of skirting can be undercut (aids snug fit to floor)

Dado and picture rails, being horizontal mouldings, may be cut and fixed using similar methods to those used for skirtings.

Start by marking a level line in the required position around the walls as shown in Figure 6.75. (Use a straight edge and spirit level or a water level and chalk line.) The required position may be related to a datum line where established.

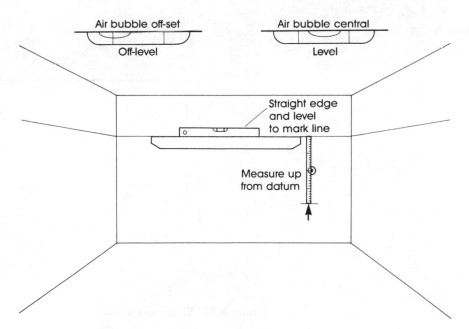

Air bubble off-set — Off-level

Air bubble central — Level

Straight edge and level to mark line

Measure up from datum

Figure 6.75 Marking positions of dado and picture rails

When working single-handed, temporary nails can be used at intervals to provide support prior to fixing (see Figure 6.76).

Simple sections can be scribed at internal corners, as are skirtings; otherwise, use mitres.

External corners should be mitred.

Fixings are normally direct to the wall surface at about 400 mm centres using typically either 50 mm cut nails or 50 mm masonry nails depending on the hardness of the wall. 50 mm oval or lost-heads can be used when fixing mouldings to timber studwork partitions.

Level line

Temporary nails to provide support during fixing

Figure 6.76 Temporary support for dado and picture rails during fixing

211

Mitres around external corners should be secured with nails through their edge. Typically 38 mm ovals or lost heads are used for this purpose.

Remember all nails should be punched below the surface.

Estimating materials

To determine the amount of trim required for any particular task is a fairly simple process, if the following procedures are used:

Architraves – The jambs or legs in most situations can be taken to be 2100 mm long. The head can be taken to be 1000 mm. These lengths assume a standard full-size door and include an allowance for mitring the ends. Thus the length of architrave required for one face of a door lining/frame is 5200 mm or 5.2 m.

Multiply this figure by the number of architrave sets to be fixed. This will determine the total metres run required, say 8 sets, both sides of four door openings,

$$5.2 \times 8 = 41.6 \text{ m}$$

Skirtings and other horizontal trim can be estimated from the perimeter. This is found by adding up the lengths of the walls in the area. The widths of any doorways and other openings are taken away to give the actual metres run required.

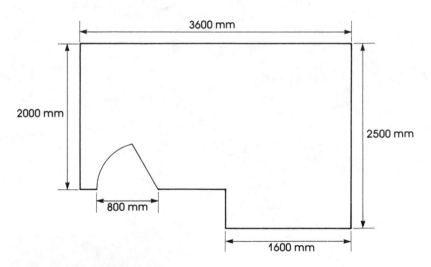

Figure 6.77 Floor plan of room

Example
Determine the total length of timber required for the room shown in Figure 6.77.

Perimeter	=	$2 + 3.6 + 2.5 + 1.6 + 0.5 + 2$
	=	12.2 m
Total metres run required	=	12.2 − 0.8 (door opening)
	=	11.4 m

An allowance of 10% for cutting and waste is normally included in any estimate for horizontal moulding.

Example
Determine the total metres run of skirting required for the run shown including an allowance of 10% for cutting and waste.

Total metres run required = 11.4 m
Total metres run required including a 10% cutting and waste allowance

$$= 11.4 + 1.14$$
$$= 12.54\,m$$
$$\text{say } 12.5\,m$$

READ THE INSTRUCTIONS AND COMPLETE THE TASK

——————— **Learning task** ———————

Determine the total metres run of skirting and dado rail required for the room shown in the diagram. Include an allowance of 10% for cutting and waste.

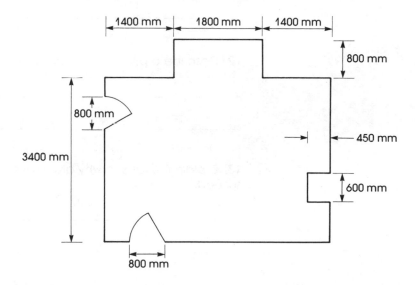

Determine the total metres run of architrave required for both faces of the doors which open into the room shown.

If you are unfamiliar with calculations or simply want to 'brush up' before attempting this learning task, refer to *Carpentry and Joinery for Advanced Students: Site Practice.*

Questions for you

9. State the purpose of using architraves and skirtings.

_____

_____

10. State the reason why a margin is left between the edge of a frame and the architrave.

_____

_____

11. State the purpose of mitring architraves.

_____

_____

12. Describe a plinth block and state where it may be used.

_____

_____

13. Explain the reason why architraves and skirtings may be scribed.

_____

_____

_____

_____

14. Produce a sketch to show a situation where a quadrant mould has been used in the place of one architrave jamb.

15. Explain why scribes are used in preference to mitres for the internal corners of skirting.

_____

_____

16. Explain the situation where heading joints may be used in skirtings.

_____

_____

17. Describe how skirting may be prepared to be fixed around a curved surface.

_____

_____

18. Describe a situation where the profile of a moulding may be returned to the wall surface.

_____

_____

19. Produce a sketch to show a torus mould to the edge of a skirting.

20. Name the fixing used to secure an architrave to a door lining.

_____

_____

WORD-SQUARE SEARCH

Hidden in the word square are the following 20 words associated with '*Finishing trim*'. You may find the words written forwards, backwards, up, down or diagonally.

Moulding	Ogee
Trim	Astragal
Skirting	Splayed
Architrave	Bullnosed
Dado rail	Scotia
Picture rail	Quadrant
Cornice	Kerfing
Scribe	Acute
Mitre	Obtuse
Ovolo	Right angle

Draw a ring around the words, or line in using a highlight pen thus:

EXAMPLE

EXAMPLE

```
P I C T U R E R A I L S O L F M C B
R U O P L G N I F R E K R A E O O U
O R R S L L M F D N D I O G M U P L
P I N L O D A E A L C R M A M L O L
R A I D V Y C N I T E T O R U D R N
I U C L O G U T T G T I S T N I T O
E A E O L P T K O O A N N S I N T S
T L W V O E E S C G L G A A C G N E
R I T O S U S Y S I P O R T A E E D
I A T R I M P E T R E S T L E T D O
G R O R I H S G I A Q H L C I S N E
H D N E L U G D O U O I E A M T E B
T R S P T N E A A C A D B N I P P I
A A T B I Y S D S R E O O I T C E R
N U O C A U R L O R G I A T R O D C
G G A L L A L D T E E R R O E C N S
L R P T N S A M E A D E D E B S I E
E S P T O D R D E V A R T I H C R A
```

Kitchen units and fitments

Units fall into two distinct categories:

Purpose made – a unit made in a joiners shop for a specific job. Most will be fully assembled prior to their arrival on site.

Proprietary – a unit or range of units mass produced to standard designs by a manufacturer. Budget-priced units are often sent in knock-down form (known as flat packs) ready for on-site assembly. Better quality units are often ready assembled (known as rigid units) in the factory.

The two main methods of construction for both proprietary and purpose-made units, shown in Figure 6.78, are box construction and framed construction.

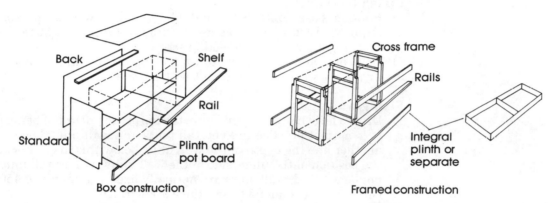

Figure 6.78 Unit construction

Box construction

This is also known as slab construction. This uses vertical standards and rails and horizontal shelves.

A back holds the unit square and rigid. The plinth and pot board are normally integral with the unit.

Proprietary units are almost exclusively made from 5 mm to 19 mm thick melamine-faced chipboard or medium density fibre board (MDF). Purpose-made units may be constructed using chipboard, MDF, block-board, melamine-faced board or, more rarely, solid timber.

Flat packs use knock down fittings or screws to join the panels. Assembly is a simple process of following the manufacturer's instructions and drawings, coupled with the ability to use a screwdriver.

Rigid and purpose-made units may be either dowelled or housed together. Glue is used on assembly to form a rigid carcass.

Framed construction

This is also known as skeleton construction. This uses frames either front and back joined by rails or standards, or cross frames joined by rails. The plinth and pot board are normally separate items.

The frames of proprietary units are normally dowelled, whereas purpose-made ones would be mortised and tenoned together.

217

Flat pack assembly and installation

The method of assembling and installing flat-pack units will vary from manufacturer to manufacturer. However, each unit is supplied with its own instructions. It is most important to take the time to read through these prior to commencing work. In general this is a three-stage process.

Assembly – Put carcases together. Unpack and assemble units one at a time and check contents. Open more than one and you risk confusing the parts!

Installation – Fix base units to the wall starting with corner base unit and working outwards from either side. Finally install wall units, again working from the corner outwards.

Finishing – Fit worktops, drawers and doors. This should not be done until all units are firmly fixed to wall and connected together.

Typical assembly instructions are shown in Figure 6.79.

Fixing base units
1) Position base units level and plumb using wedges provided if required. Ensure all top edges and fronts of units are flush. Secure units together using connecting screws.
2) Drill, plug and screw units to wall, using the brackets provided.
3) Trim floor wedges flush to unit with a knife.

Fixing wall units
1) Draw a level horizontal line from the top of the tall unit if being used. It is normal practice to keep tall units and wall units level. Draw another line the depth of the wall units below this line. This marks the position of the underside of the wall units. Where tall units are not being used, wall units are normally fixed with a gap of 450 mm between their underside and the work surface.
2) Temporarily fix a batten on the marked level line, to act as a support while marking fixing holes and screwing.
3) Rest the unit on the batten. Ensure the tops of wall units and tall units are flush.
4) Mark the wall through the fixing holes.
5) Drill, plug and screw the unit to the wall.
6) Packing behind a fixing may be required on an uneven wall surface to ensure the units are plumb.
7) Position the remaining wall units in place one at a time.
8) Ensure the top edges and fronts are flush and secure together using connecting screws.

Fixing worktops
1) Measure and cut the worktop to the required size. (Post formed, see 'Worktops' on p. 220 for other types.)
2) Metal filler/joint strips are used to connect worktops in corners.
3) Position worktop and screw in place through the fixing brackets.
4) Sawn bare ends of the top can be covered with a metal trim or a plastic pre-glued edge banding. Iron edge banding into place, using a sheet of paper in between banding and iron for protection.

Fixing drawers – Insert drawers, made up previously, onto drawer runners.

Fixing doors
1) Lay the doors face down on a flat clean surface.
2) Locate the hinges over the previously fixed hinge plate and secure with a mounting screw.
3) Adjust the hinges if required to ensure accurate door alignment.

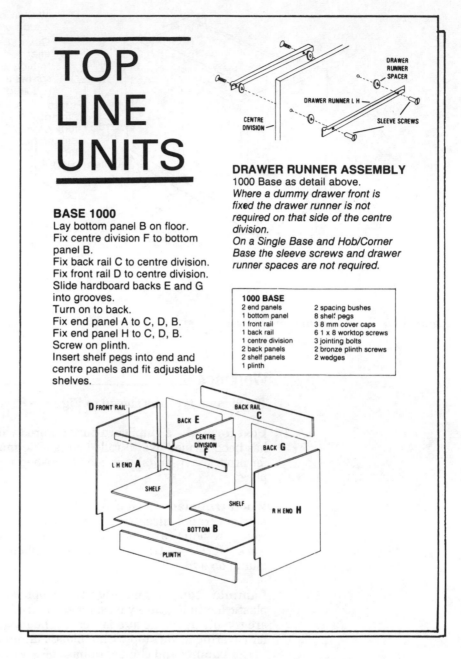

TOP LINE UNITS

BASE 1000
Lay bottom panel B on floor.
Fix centre division F to bottom panel B.
Fix back rail C to centre division.
Fix front rail D to centre division.
Slide hardboard backs E and G into grooves.
Turn on to back.
Fix end panel A to C, D, B.
Fix end panel H to C, D, B.
Screw on plinth.
Insert shelf pegs into end and centre panels and fit adjustable shelves.

DRAWER RUNNER ASSEMBLY
1000 Base as detail above.
Where a dummy drawer front is fixed the drawer runner is not required on that side of the centre division.
On a Single Base and Hob/Corner Base the sleeve screws and drawer runner spaces are not required.

1000 BASE	
2 end panels	2 spacing bushes
1 bottom panel	8 shelf pegs
1 front rail	3 8 mm cover caps
1 back rail	6 1 x 8 worktop screws
1 centre division	3 jointing bolts
2 back panels	2 bronze plinth screws
2 shelf panels	2 wedges
1 plinth	

Figure 6.79 Typical manufacturer's assembly instructions

Rigid and purpose-made installation

The installation of rigid and purpose-made units follows the general procedures used for flat-pack units.

Good quality rigid units have adjustable legs for easier levelling on an uneven floor. In addition wall units often have adjustable wall brackets which enable fine adjustment to plumb and level.

Purpose-made units often have provision for scribing to uneven floor and wall surfaces (see Figure 6.80).

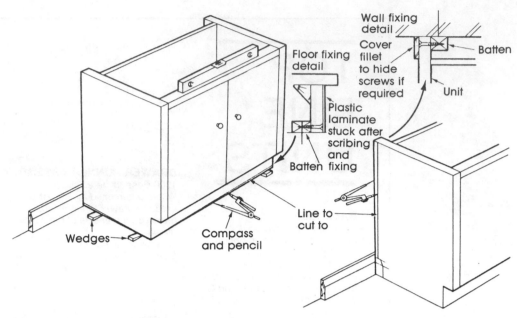

Figure 6.80 Scribing to uneven surfaces

Worktops

Three main types as shown in Figure 6.81 are in common use:

Post formed – a chipboard base covered with a plastic laminate which has been formed over a rolled edge. The most popular type of worktop for proprietary units, it is ready finished and simply requires fixing in place.

Wood trimmed – a chipboard base covered with either a plastic laminate or ceramic tiles. A hardwood trim is tongued and glued to the front edge, providing a neat finish. This is mainly used for higher quality work. Hardwood trim is normally supplied loose, ready for mitring and gluing on site.

Laminate topped and edged – a chipboard base edged and covered in plastic laminate, rarely used for standard jobs, as post-formed worktops are readily available at a low cost. The following procedure can be used for covering a worktop with a plastic laminate.

1) Fix units and chipboard base of worktop in position.
2) Cut edging strips. This can best be done by setting a marking or cutting gauge to the required width and running it along the edge of the laminate to score its surface. The strip is separated by applying thumb pressure along the score, at the same time lifting up the edge of the strip.

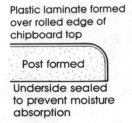

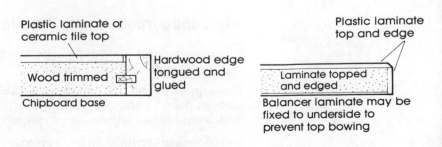

Figure 6.81 Worktops

3) Stick on edging strips with contact adhesive, following the manufacturer's recommendations.

Note: Two coats of adhesive should be applied to the edge of the worktop. The first acts as a primer to seal the absorbent surface.

4) File all the edges and corners to a neat finish.

5) Cut top laminate slightly over the required size. This can be done by scoring the sheet with a laminate cutter and breaking the sheet upwards along the scored line.

6) Thoroughly dust off the work surface and the back of the laminate. Apply a contact adhesive to both surfaces and allow to become touch dry.

7) Lay small prepared strips of timber on the work surface at about 150 mm intervals. Place the laminate sheet on top of the strips.

8) Ensuring that the laminate is correctly positioned, remove the strips one at a time and press the laminate down onto the top, working from the centre to the edge of the sheet each time to avoid air traps.

Note: The purpose of the timber strips is to separate the two surfaces until they are correctly located. A sheet of building paper can be used instead of strips. This is progressively pulled out as the laminate is pressed down.

9) Apply pressure to the surface by rubbing down from the centre with the palm of the hand.

10) Trim the edges, preferably using a powered router. Where this is not available a file, block plane or cabinet scraper can be used.

Questions for you

21. Describe the difference between flat-pack and rigid proprietary kitchen units.

_____

_____

_____

22. Produce a sketch to show the following **THREE** worktop edge details:
(a) post formed
(b) wood trimmed
(c) laminate edged

23. Name the adhesive used for bonding plastic laminate to a work surface.

_____

24. A kitchen is to be fitted with a range of units to form an L shape. Describe the sequence in which these units should be fixed.

_____

_____

_____

Panelling and cladding

Panelling

Wall panelling is the general term given to the covering of internal wall surfaces and sometimes ceilings, with timber or other materials to create a decorative finish. All panelling may be classified by its height and method of construction.

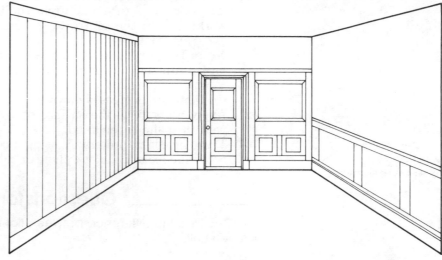

Figure 6.82 Panelling

Heights of panelling

Dado height panelling – extends from the floor up the walls to the window sill level or chair back height, i.e. about 1 m above the floor.

Three-quarter height panelling – also known as frieze height panelling. It extends from the floor up the walls to the top of the door, i.e about 2 m. Traditionally a plate shelf was incorporated on top of this type of panelling to display plates and other frieze ornaments.

Full height panelling – as its name suggests, covers the whole of the wall from floor to ceiling.

Construction of panelling

Traditional panelling consists of stiles, rails and muntins, mortised and tenoned together, with panels infilled between the framing members, which are themselves fixed back to grounds. In modern usage the term panelling is also loosely applied to wall linings made up of sheet material, or matchboarding.

Grounds – provide a flat and level surface on which the panelling can be fixed (see Figure 6.84). They are normally preservative-treated softwood and may have been framed up using halvings or mortise and tenon joints or, alternatively, supplied in lengths for use as separate grounds or counter battening (a double layer fixed at right angles).

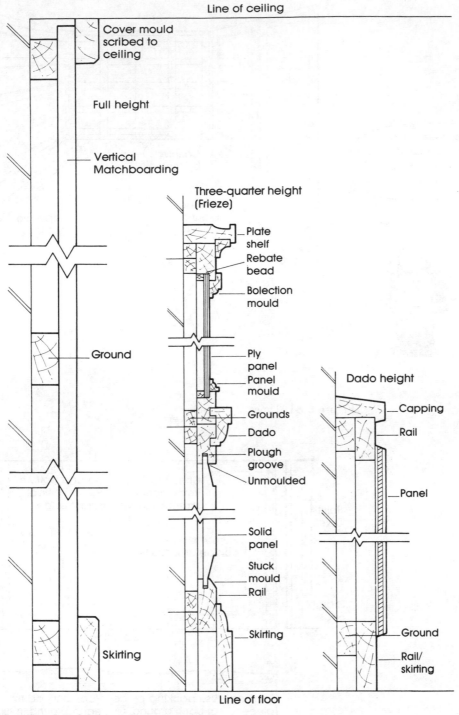

Figure 6.83 Panelling heights

Grounds are fixed back to the wall surface either by

- plugging and screwing,
- cut-nailing into the mortar joint or brickwork
- cut-nailing direct into the surface of blockwork,
- nailing direct into the brickwork using hardened nails or by using cartridge fixing tools. (Goggles for eye protection should be worn.)

They must be plumbed and lined in to provide a flat surface (see Figure 6.85).

Fixing to grounds – the fixing of panelling to grounds should as far as possible be concealed.

223

GROUNDS MUST BE PLUMBED, LEVELLED AND LINED-IN TO ENSURE A FLAT FIXING SURFACE

Figure 6.84 Types of grounds

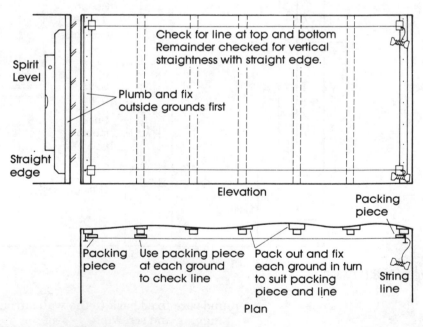

Figure 6.85 Plumbing and lining grounds

Panelling should be lowered into position and held in place by interlocking grounds, one fixed to the wall and the other to the panelling (see Figure 6.86).

Interlocking metal plates or keyhole slots and screws also provide a fixing when the panelling is lowered into position. Cover fillets or other trim may be used to conceal panelling that has been surface screwed.

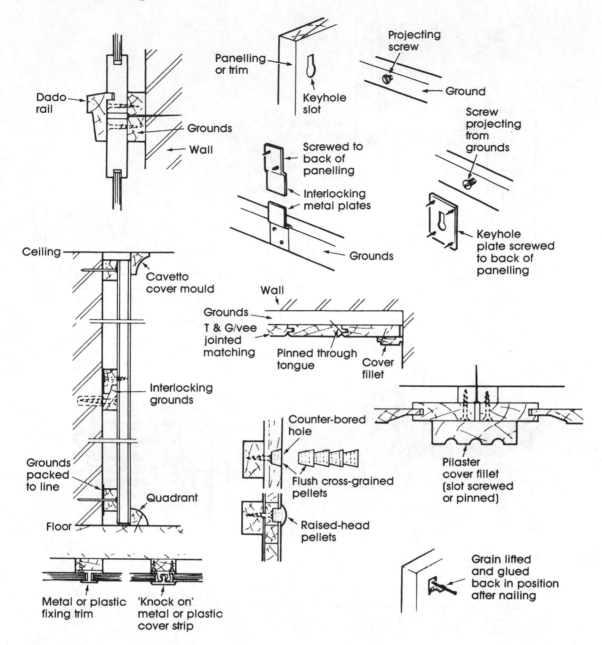

Figure 6.86 Concealed fixings

Corner details – the method of forming internal and external angles will depend on the type of panelling, but in any case they should be adequately supported by grounds fixed behind. Figure 6.87 shows various details. Tongued-and-grooved joints, loose tongues, rebates or cover fillets and trims have been used to locate the panelling members and at the same time conceal the effects of moisture movement.

Where matchboarding or similar timber strips are used for panelling, the boards at either end of a wall should be of equal width (see Figure 6.88).

A simple calculation can be carried out to determine the required width.

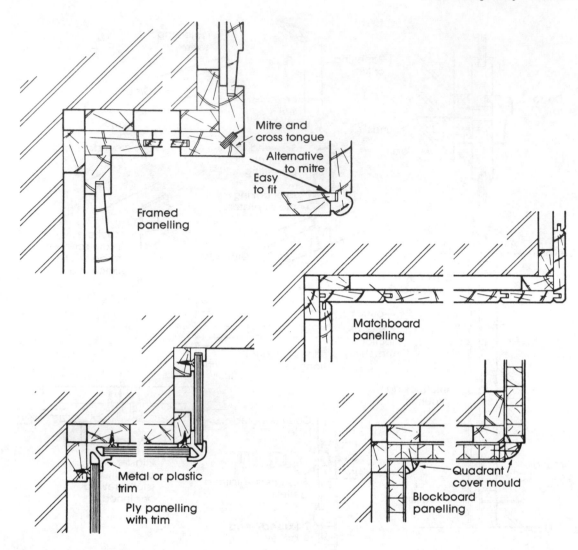

Figure 6.87 Corner details

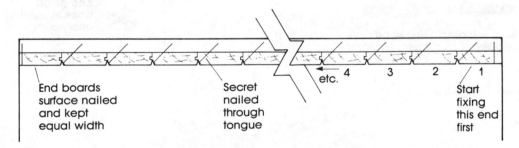

Figure 6.88 Layout of matchboard panelling

Example

3.114 m length of wall is to be panelled with 95 mm (90 mm covering width) matchboard.

Divide the length of wall in millimetres by the covering width of the board.

$3114 \div 90 = 34.6$ boards

Therefore 35 boards are required: 33 whole boards and two cut end boards.

Width of cut end boards $= \dfrac{1.6 \times 90}{2}$

$= 72$ mm

General requirements of panelling

1) Before any panelling commences it is essential that the wall construction has dried sufficiently.
2) All timber should be of the moisture content required for the respective situation (equilibrium moisture content, M/C).
3) The backs of the panelling sections should be sealed prior to fixing, thus preventing moisture absorption.
4) Timber for grounds should be preservative treated.
5) A ventilated air space is desirable between the panelling and the wall.
6) Provision must be made for a slight amount of moisture movement in both the panelling sections and the trim.
7) The positioning of the grounds must be planned to suit the panelling.
8) The fixing of the panelling to the grounds should be so designed that it is concealed as far as possible.

Cladding

Cladding is the non-loadbearing skin or covering of external walls for weathering purposes, e.g. timber boarding, sheet material, tile hanging and cement rendering.

Timber cladding for either timber-framed buildings or those of brick or blockwork construction is fixed to battens or grounds spaced at a maximum of 600 mm centres. A moisture barrier is fixed below the cladding to battens in timber-framed buildings to provide a second line of protection to any wind-driven rain that might penetrate the cladding. This is often termed a breather paper, as it must allow the warm air vapour to pass or breath through it from inside the building and not get trapped in the wall. The moisture barrier is often omitted for claddings over brick or blockwork.

The battens are fixed to the studs of the timber frame or direct to the brick or block surface. They must be lined and levelled to provide a flat surface.

Cladding is normally specified as 16 mm. Feather-edged boards will taper to about 6 mm at their thin edge. Natural durable timber cladding such as Western Red Cedar may be used without preservative treatment or any subsequent finish. Most other softwood claddings are not naturally durable and must be preservative treated.

ONLY ONE NAIL PER BOARD WIDTH IN ORDER TO REDUCE THE LIKELIHOOD OF SPLITTING AFTER MOISTURE MOVEMENT

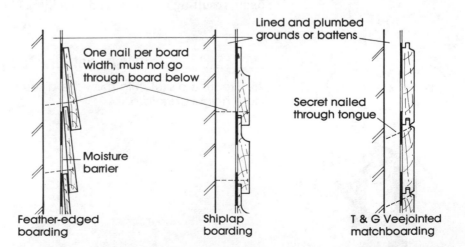

Figure 6.89 Types of cladding

227

It is recommended that all timber used for cladding, the grounds as well as the boarding, is preservative treated before use. There is little point in treating the face of cladding after it has been fixed, leaving the joints or overlapping areas, back faces and grounds untreated. Any preservative-treated timber cut to size on site will require re-treatment on the freshly cut ends and edges. This can be carried out by applying two brush flood coats of preservative.

Timber is a hygroscopic material, it readily absorbs or gives off moisture to achieve a balance with its surroundings. In doing so it expands or shrinks. Cladding sections should be designed to minimise, mask or cover and unsightly gaps resulting from moisture movement (see Figure 6.90).

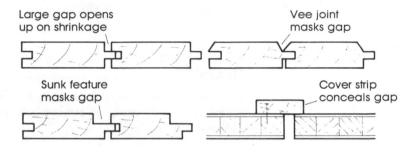

Large gap opens up on shrinkage

Vee joint masks gap

Sunk feature masks gap

Cover strip conceals gap

Figure 6.90 Effects of moisture movement and the remedy

Fixings – are normally nails at least $2\frac{1}{2}$ times in length the cladding's thickness. Ferrous metal (metal that will rust) nails should be galvanised or sherardised to resist corrosion. Copper or aluminium nails must be used with Western Red Cedar as it accelerates rusting in ferrous metals and causes unsightly timber staining.

Plywood used for cladding must be WBP rated. This means that its veneer layers have been glued using a weather and boilproof adhesive to give it a very high resistance to all weather conditions.

Fibreboard or hardboard must be of the oil tempered kind for weather resistance. Before fixing, hardboard sheets will require conditioning. This involves brushing up to one litre of water into the back face (rough surface) of each sheet 24 to 48 hours before fixing. The purpose of conditioning is to expand the sheet which ensures that it dries out and shrinks on its fixings and remains flat. If this were not done it could expand after fixing resulting in a bowing or buckling of the surface.

TRY TO ANSWER THESE

Questions for you

25. Produce a sketch to show the difference between dado and frieze height panelling.

26. Explain why grounds must be plumbed and lined in.

_____

_____

27. Explain why exterior plywood cladding should be specified as WBP rated.

_____

_____

28. Explain the reason for using copper nails when fixing Western Red Cedar cladding.

_____

_____

29. State the purpose of the vee joint in matchboard panelling.

_____

_____

30. State the purpose of incorporating a moisture barrier below external timber cladding.

_____

_____

31. State a reason why Western Red Cedar may be specified for external cladding.

_____

_____

32. Produce a sketch to show how wall panelling may be secret fixed using splayed grounds.

33. Describe the conditioning of hardboard prior to fixing, and state why this process is carried out.

_____

_____

_____

WELL, HOW DID YOU DO?

WORK THROUGH THE SECTION AGAIN IF YOU HAD ANY PROBLEMS

WORD-SQUARE SEARCH

Hidden in the word square are the following 20 words associated with '*Paneling and cladding*'. You may find the words written forwards, backwards, up, down or diagonally.

Panel	Cladding
Dado	Stile
Ground	Vapour
Batten	Breather
Rebate	Preservative
Matchboarding	Feather edge
Frieze	Levelled
Tongue	Conditioning
Groove	Hygroscopic
Interlocking	Keyhole

Draw a ring round the words, or line in using a highlight pen thus:

EXAMPLE

EXAMPLE

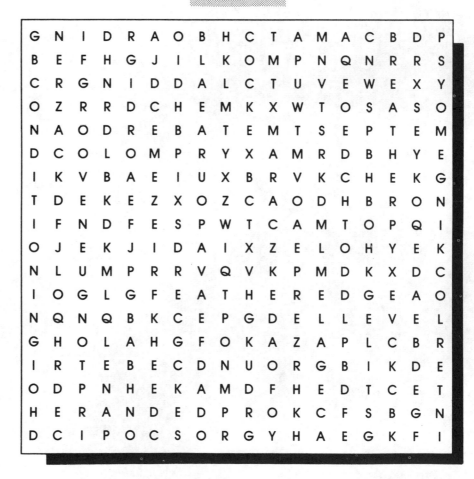

Index